# Volume II
# QUICK & EASY
# CHRISTMAS
# CRAFTS

164 projects for gifts,
ornaments and holiday
decorating

D1378763

The publishers and designers wish to thank the following companies for providing materials used in this publication:

- **Adhesive Technologies, Inc.** for Craft & Floral Pro™ low temperature glue guns and sticks
- **Aldastar Corp.** for pom poms
- **Aleene's** for tacky craft glue and washable fabric glue
- **All Cooped Up Designs** for curly crepe wool doll hair
- **Artifacts, Inc.** for tassels
- **B. B. World Corporation** for mini paper roses
- **Canson-Talens, Inc.** for photo albums
- **Carnival Arts, Inc.** for spray paints, spray glitter, spray webbing and spray adhesive
- **C. M. Offray & Son, Inc.** for ribbons, ribbon roses and ribbon poinsettias
- **Creative Beginnings** for brass charms
- **Darice, Inc.** for wooden shapes, doll heads and stands
- **Decorator & Craft Corporation** for papier-mâché boxes
- **DecoArt** for acrylic paints and crackle medium
- **Delta Technical Coatings, Inc.** for acrylic paints, dimensional paints, sealers and varnishes
- **Design Master Color Tool, Inc.** for spray paints
- **Duncan Enterprises** for dimensional paints
- **Fiskars, Inc.** for decorative edge scissors
- **Flora Craft** for Styrofoam® and floral foams
- **Forster, Inc.** for wooden items
- **International Flower Importers** for preserved greens
- **Jesse M. James & Co.** for buttons
- **Libbey, Inc.** for bottles
- **Lion Ribbon Company** for ribbons
- **Luzon Imports** for TWIGS™ items
- **Mill Store Products, Inc.** for birdhouses, wooden items
- **Modern Forge** for hurricane lamps
- **MPR Associates Inc.** for paper and mylar ribbons
- **Novtex Corp.** for braids and trims
- **One & Only Creations** for curly doll hair
- **Peking Handicrafts, Inc.** for doilies
- **Plaid Enterprises, Inc.** for dimensional fabric paints
- **Schusters of Texas** for dried and preserved flowers
- **Robert Simmons, Inc.** for paintbrushes
- **The Spice Market, Inc.** for dried roses, potpourri and cinnamon sticks
- **St. Louis Trimming Inc.** for trims and laces
- **Sweet Antiques Inc.** for glass bottles
- **Teters Floral Products** for silk flowers and greens
- **Walnut Hollow Farm, Inc.** for birdhouses, wooden items
- **Wangs International Inc.** for bells, garlands, silk flowers, crocheted lace, straw and abaca items, baskets, buttons, plaster wall sconce and the birch-wrapped wreath
- **Wimpole Street Creations, Inc.** for doilies and fabric yo-yos
- **Winward Silks** for silk flowers and greens
- **Wrights** for ribbons, trims and laces

**Styrofoam®** is a registered trademark of Dow Chemical Corporation.
**Fimo®** is a registered trademark of Eberhard Faber GmbH, EFA-Str. 1, 92318 Neumarkt/Germany.

published by

in association with

and

Library of Congress Catalog Card Number 96-69844
Hardcover ISBN 0-8487-1560-8
Softcover ISBN 0-8487-1564-0

Printed in the United States of America
First printing 1997

**Oxmoor House**
**Editor-in-Chief:** Nancy Fitzpatrick Wyatt
**Senior Crafts Editor:** Susan Ramey Cleveland
**Senior Editor, Editorial Services:** Olivia K. Wells
**Art Director:** James Boone

**Hot Off The Press, Inc.**
**Project Editor:** Mary Margaret Hite
**Technical Editors:** Terry Dolney, LeNae Gerig, Lisa Klupenger
**Photographers:** Meredith Marsh, Susannah Roth
**Graphic Designer:** Sally Clarke, Jacie Pete
**Digital Imagers:** Michael Kincaid, Larry Seith
**Editors:** Paulette McCord Jarvey, Teresa Nelson, Tom Muir

1 2 3 4 5 6 7 8 9

## Volume II

# QUICK & EASY
# CHRISTMAS
# CRAFTS

### 164 projects for gifts, ornaments and holiday decorating

# Table of Contents

## Decorate To Celebrate

## Romantic Accents

## Quick & Easy Gifts

## Tree Treasures

# Whimsical Buddies & Pals

# Wrap It Up!

# Hints, Tips & Techniques

# Decorate To Celebrate

Imagine decorating your home for the Christmas holidays with swags, garlands, ornaments and wreaths, all coordinated to your favorite theme. Our designers have created wonderful decorations for your home in four distinctive themes.

The Nostalgic theme includes Santas, elves and snowmen, all in bright greens and reds. They brighten even the darkest corner of a room and bring a traditional Christmas feeling to any home. The charming Ho Ho Ho Banner on page 22 is sure to make kids and adults smile when hung on a door or near the Christmas tree.

A Natural theme is represented by designs featuring greenery, fruit, dried wheat, bark, mosses, birds and a birdhouse. The Birch-Wrapped Wreath, page 17, brings a bit of the outdoors inside, providing a feeling of Christmas in the forest. The Fruit Arch & Candle Rings from page 18 add richness with gold ribbon, while still keeping the natural feeling provided by the wheat and fruit.

Lace, eucalyptus, roses and ribbons bedeck the designs in the Romantic theme on pages 12-15, while magnolias mixed with evergreens and ribbons distinguish the Elegant theme on pages 8-11.

Once the designs for a certain theme are created, it's easy to use the same or similar components to carry it throughout the entire home. With the festive and stunning projects provided here and because of their easy construction, we know you'll enjoy decorating your home for the holidays!

# BERIBBONED WREATH

by LeNae Gerig

20" round vinyl pine wreath
2 yards of 4" wide ivory/gold wire-edged
 ribbon
3 yards of ⅝" wide white/gold trim
1 ivory/gold silk floral pick with one 6" wide
 magnolia blossom, one 3" wide dogwood
 blossom, clusters of many ⅜"–½" gold
 berries, many 1½"–4" leaves and tendrils
five 12" long cone picks with three 3"–5"
 sprigs of ¼"–½" wide gold balls, tendrils
 and many ½" wide glittered cones
five 2½" wide gold glass Christmas balls
gold glitter spray
low temperature glue gun and sticks
24-gauge wire

1 Use the ribbon to make an oblong bow (see page 140) with a center loop, six 3"–4" loops, a 6" tail and a 9" tail. Glue to the wreath at 11:00. Weave the 9" tail among the pine sprigs on the left and the 6" tail to the right. Cut the dogwood and magnolia blossoms off the pick, making the dogwood a 7" sprig and the magnolia a 5" sprig. Glue the dogwood to the left and the magnolia to the right of the bow.

2 Cut five 9" lengths of white/gold trim and glue each length around the center of a gold ball. Glue the balls evenly spaced around the wreath, turning them at varying angles. Glue one end of the remaining white/gold trim under the bow, then loop it among the balls, tucking and gluing it among the pine sprigs. Glue the other end under the other side of the bow.

3 Cut the sprigs off the cone picks. Glue them around the bow and evenly spaced among the balls as shown.

4 Spray the wreath with gold glitter; let dry. Use the wire to make a loop hanger (see page 144) at the top back.

# HURRICANE CENTERPIECE
by Anne-Marie Spencer

1 hurricane lamp with a 4½" wide base and 8" chimney
one 8" round vine wreath
1⅓ yards of 2½" wide white net ribbon with 4 gold wires
  on each side
2 green PVC pine picks, each with twenty-six 5" branches
2 stems of gold silk poinsettias, each with one 8" wide
  blossom
2 stems of gold latex grapes, each with three 3" long clusters
  of many ½" wide grapes
2 green/gold picks, each with a 1" square gift, 2" long pine
  cone, 1¼" apple and 1 cluster of many ½" long silk
  leaves
2 stems of white silk spirea, each with fifteen 1" wide clusters of many ¼" wide blossoms and many 1½"–2½"
  long leaves
2 oz. of gold-painted curly twigs
low temperature glue gun and sticks

1 Insert the lamp base snugly into the center of the
wreath. Cut the pine into 5"–7" sprigs and glue
evenly spaced into the wreath as shown, placing the 7"
sprigs on opposite sides to create an oval shape.

2 Cut the poinsettia stems to 2"; glue one on each
long side near the lamp base. Cut the spirea into
fourteen 3"–6" sprigs. Glue them evenly spaced around
the wreath with longer sprigs on the long sides.

3 Cut the grapes into six 4" sprigs; glue three to each
side evenly spaced as shown. Glue a gift/cone pick
into the front and one into the back (see arrows).

4 Cut the ribbon into four 12" lengths. Glue one in
front of and one behind each poinsettia, angling
toward the sides. Cut the twigs into 5" sprigs and glue
evenly spaced among the previous materials.

# WALL SCONCE
## by Anne-Marie Spencer

one 9" tall gilded plaster wall sconce
3 green PVC pine picks, each with twenty-six 5"
    long branches
1 stem of white latex lilies with two 7" wide
    blossoms, 2 buds and three 6" long leaves
2 stems of white silk roses, each with five 1" wide
    blossoms, 3 buds and many 1" leaves
3 stems of white silk vervain, each with three 7"
    wide blossoms
1 stem of gold latex twigs with 5 branches of
    8"–12" twigs
4 oz. of green preserved cedar
two 4" long pine cones
4 oz. of gold glittered preserved holly leaves
1 oz. of green sheet moss
5½"x3"x3" block of floral foam for drieds
low temperature glue gun and sticks

1 Glue the foam to the top of the sconce; trim the
   corners so it doesn't extend past the sconce front.
Cut the pine picks into 6"–9" sprigs and glue them
evenly spaced into the foam. Glue moss as needed to
conceal the foam. Cut the cedar into 6" sprigs and glue
evenly spaced among the pine sprigs.

2 Cut the lily stem into one 5" sprig with one blossom and one 14" sprig with with one blossom and
two buds. Glue the 14" sprig into the top of the foam
and the 5" sprig to the right front of the first, angling
the blossoms toward the front. Cut each rose stem into
one 9" and one 6" sprig. Glue a 9" sprig right of the top
lily, angling up and outward. Glue a 6" sprig below it at
the same angle. Glue a 9" sprig angling outward from
the center left and a 6" sprig extending forward from
the center front.

3 Cut the twigs into five 8"–12" sprigs and glue evenly spaced among the previous materials as shown.
Glue the pine cones to the left and right of the lilies.

4 Cut the holly into 5" sprigs and glue evenly spaced
   among all the materials. Cut the vervain into nine
9" sprigs and glue as for the holly, angling the blossoms
downward.

# MAGNOLIA GARLAND

by
Anne-Marie
Spencer

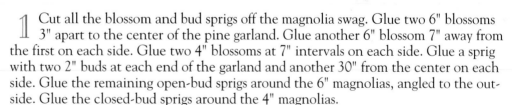

one 9' long green PVC pine garland with many 5" long sprigs

4 yards of 3" wide gold lamé wire-edged ribbon

one 36" long magnolia swag with four 6" and four 4" wide blossoms, eleven 1"–2" wide open buds, 6 closed buds and many 5"–7" long leaves

six 3" wide gold plastic ball ornaments

3 stems of pearl grapes, each with three 3" long clusters of many ½" white grapes

2 stems of white silk snowberries, each with four 2-branched sections containing 3 clusters of many ⅛" berries

4 oz. of gold-painted curly twigs

6 oz. of gold-painted preserved holly

low temperature glue gun and sticks

1 Cut all the blossom and bud sprigs off the magnolia swag. Glue two 6" blossoms 3" apart to the center of the pine garland. Glue another 6" blossom 7" away from the first on each side. Glue two 4" blossoms at 7" intervals on each side. Glue a sprig with two 2" buds at each end of the garland and another 30" from the center on each side. Glue the remaining open-bud sprigs around the 6" magnolias, angled to the outside. Glue the closed-bud sprigs around the 4" magnolias.

2 Weave the ribbon loosely among the magnolias and pine sprigs as shown, gluing to secure it as needed and at each end. Glue the gold balls evenly spaced throughout the garland.

3 Cut the grapes into nine 4" sprigs and glue them evenly spaced throughout the garland, with the sprigs left of center angled left and the sprigs right of center angled right. Cut the holly into 5" sprigs and glue evenly spaced, angled as for the grapes.

4 Cut the twigs into 6"–8" sprigs and the snowberries into 4" sprigs. Glue them evenly spaced as for the grapes and holly.

# LACE & ROSES EUCALYPTUS SWAG

by Karin
Hupp

one 5" wide white battenburg lace hat
1¼ yards of ⅝" wide gold/red metallic ribbon with 3mm
    white fused pearl trim
2 stems of burgundy silk roses, each with six ¾"–1" wide
    blossoms
1 stem of white silk wildflowers with 13 sprigs, each with
    6 clusters of five ⅛" wide blossoms
4 oz. of dark green preserved eucalyptus
4 oz. of green preserved cedar
2 oz. of dried German statice
six 1½" long gold pine cones
24-gauge wire
low temperature glue gun and sticks

Glue the rest evenly spaced among the eucalyptus. Cut
the wildflowers into one 6" and eleven 4" sprigs. Glue
the 6" and one 4" sprig under the right side of the hat
angled down over the cedar sprig. Glue four 4" sprigs 1"
apart on each side of the hat, following the angles of the
cedar and eucalyptus. Glue two 4" sprigs to the right hat
brim extending upward and downward as shown.

3 Cut the roses into one 4" sprig of three blossoms
  and nine one-blossom sprigs. Glue the 4" sprig to
the right of the hat extending downward over the cedar
sprig. Glue the remaining roses over the wildflowers as
shown. Cut the German statice into 4" sprigs and glue
evenly spaced among the roses and wildflowers.

4 Glue two cones on each side of the hat and two
  among the downward-angled florals. Cut a 13" ribbon length and make a collar bow (see page 140) with
2" loops and 2½" tails. Glue to the hat at 11:00, angled
as shown. Cut the remaining ribbon into two 13" and
two 15" tails. On each side, glue a 15" tail above a 13"
tail. Loop and glue each end as shown.

1 Separate the eucalyptus into two equal bunches, overlap the stems and wire to form a swag. Reinforce the
wire with glue. Attach a wire loop hanger (see page 144) to
the top back. Glue the hat to the swag center.

2 Cut the cedar into 6"–10" sprigs. Glue one sprig
  under the right side of the hat, angled downward.

# CANDLE RING OR WREATH

### by LeNae Gerig

20" wide sunburst twig wreath with a 6" opening
1 stem of green silk pine with twelve 4"–5" sprigs
2⅔ yards of 1⅜" wide burgundy grosgrain ribbon
four 6" wide white crocheted doilies
⅞ yard of 2½" wide burgundy/green/gold wire-edged ribbon
1 oz. of blue-green preserved eucalyptus
1 oz. of white dried glittered German statice
1 oz. of light green plumosus
four ⅜" wide burgundy ribbon roses with green leaves
8"x2½" wide white pillar candle
22-gauge wire
low temperature glue gun and sticks

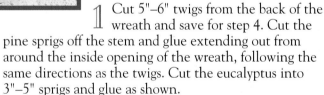

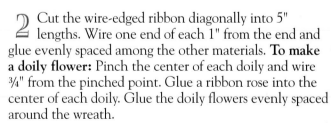

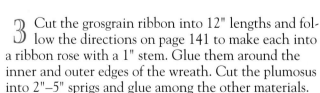

1 Cut 5"–6" twigs from the back of the wreath and save for step 4. Cut the pine sprigs off the stem and glue extending out from around the inside opening of the wreath, following the same directions as the twigs. Cut the eucalyptus into 3"–5" sprigs and glue as shown.

2 Cut the wire-edged ribbon diagonally into 5" lengths. Wire one end of each 1" from the end and glue evenly spaced among the other materials. **To make a doily flower:** Pinch the center of each doily and wire ¾" from the pinched point. Glue a ribbon rose into the center of each doily. Glue the doily flowers evenly spaced around the wreath.

3 Cut the grosgrain ribbon into 12" lengths and follow the directions on page 141 to make each into a ribbon rose with a 1" stem. Glue them around the inner and outer edges of the wreath. Cut the plumosus into 2"–5" sprigs and glue among the other materials.

4 Cut the statice into 2"–3" sprigs. Glue the twigs from step 1 and the statice evenly spaced among the other materials. Lay the wreath flat and place the candle in the center of the wreath (or see page 144 to wire a hanger at the top back to use as a wreath).

# MANTEL GARLAND by Anne-Marie Spencer

one 54" long green PVC pine garland
2 yards of 3" wide burgundy/green/gold print ribbon
four 2" wide white ribbon roses
5 stems of burgundy silk roses, each with one 4" wide blossom
3 stems of burgundy silk vervain, each with three 7" long blossom clusters
1 stem of gold latex twigs with 3 sections of ten 10" long sprigs
4 oz. of green preserved spiral eucalyptus
4 oz. of mint green preserved plumosus
4 oz. of preserved baby's breath
24-gauge wire
low temperature glue gun and sticks

1 Fluff the garland sprigs. Cut the eucalyptus into 5" sprigs and glue evenly spaced among the pine sprigs, with those right of center angled to the right and those left of center angled to the left.

2 Cut the stems off the silk roses and glue them evenly spaced among the pine and eucalyptus sprigs. Glue the ribbon roses evenly spaced between the silk roses.

3 Cut the plumosus into 5" sprigs and the vervain into 7" sprigs. Glue evenly spaced among the previous materials.

4 Cut the baby's breath and twigs into 5" sprigs and glue as for the plumosus and vervain. Cut the ribbon into six 6" lengths. Trim one end of each length diagonally. Gather and wire the straight ends. Glue the wired ends evenly spaced into the garland, following the angles of the previous materials.

# HEARTH BASKET

by Anne-Marie Spencer

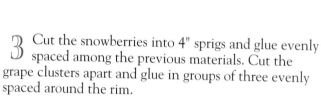

*one 13"x18" oval whitewashed
  willow basket with an 8" tall
  handle*
*6⅓ yards of ⅛" wide burgundy
  rope braid*
*four 18" long green PVC pine
  boughs, each with three 9"
  branches of many 5" sprigs*
*4 stems of burgundy silk roses,
  each with one 4" wide
  blossom*
*2 stems of white silk snow-
  berries, each with nine 4"
  sprigs of many 1/16" berries*
*3 gold latex grape picks, each
  with many ½" wide grapes*
*4 oz. of green preserved eucalyptus*
*4 oz. of burgundy dried glittered German statice*
*3 oz. of mint green preserved plumosus*
*four 6" round white crocheted doilies*
*22-gauge wire*
*low temperature glue gun and sticks*

1 Cut the branches off the pine and glue them
  around the rim of the basket, angling them counterclockwise and fluffing the sprigs. Cut the eucalyptus
into 5" lengths and glue among the pine sprigs at similar angles.

2 Cut the stems off the roses; glue one into the center of each doily. Glue the doilies evenly spaced
along the basket rim. Cut the plumosus into 5" sprigs
and glue evenly spaced among the pine and eucalyptus.

3 Cut the snowberries into 4" sprigs and glue evenly
  spaced among the previous materials. Cut the
grape clusters apart and glue in groups of three evenly
spaced around the rim.

4 Cut the statice into 4" sprigs and glue evenly
  spaced around the rim. Cut a 36" braid length and
wrap it spiral fashion around the handle with the wraps
4" apart. Cut two 36" lengths and use each to make a
loopy bow (see page 140) with four 3" loops and 6"
tails. Glue one to each handle base; untwist the tails.
Cut two 5" braid lengths, untwist and glue one below
each bow as an extra tail. Drape the remaining braid
around the basket, going twice around and gluing it to
the rim bottom every quarter turn.

# BIRCH BIRDHOUSE

### by Anne-Marie Spencer

*one 8"x8"x6" wooden birdhouse*
*two 6"x5" pieces of birch bark*
*granite Fleck Stone™ spray paint*
*acrylic spray sealer*
*1 oz. of green preserved princess pine*
*1 oz. of red dried canella*
*1 oz. of white preserved ti tree*
*eleven ¾"–1¼" long pine cones*
*1 oz. of dried forest coral lichen*
*1 oz. of dwarf's beard moss*
*one 2" long mushroom bird*
*low temperature glue gun and sticks*

1 Spray the birdhouse, except the roof, with Fleck Stone™. Let dry and coat with sealer. Glue the birch bark to the roof; glue dwarf's beard moss to cover the seam.

2 Break the remaining moss into fine 4" lengths and glue along the eaves of the roof and around the base. Break the lichen into 1" tufts. Glue a tuft to the perch, one into the door hole and the rest at 1" to 2" intervals into the moss.

3 Cut the ti tree into 1"–3" sprigs. Glue a cluster of five to each front corner of the base; repeat at 3" intervals around the base. Cut a 3" pine sprig and glue at the top back corner of the left roof, extending downward. Cut the remaining pine into 2" sprigs and glue evenly spaced around the base. Glue two cones to the base of the 3" sprig and one near each remaining pine sprig.

4 Cut the canella into 1" sprigs. Glue one sprig between the cones on the roof and the rest evenly spaced around the base. Glue the bird into the door hole, facing out.

1

2

3

4

# BIRCH-WRAPPED WREATH

by Anne-Marie Spencer

*one 16" round wreath wrapped in birch bark\**
*one 24" long green PVC pine pick with 2 branches of many 5" sprigs*
*4 oz. of preserved blueberry juniper*
*3 oz. of dried barley*
*3 oz. of red dried pepperberries*
*2 oz. of 2"–4" long red dried chili peppers*
*3 dried pomegranates*
*five 2" long pine cones*
*8 dried apple slices*
*24-gauge wire*
*low temperature glue gun and sticks*

*\*or wrap a 16" Styrofoam® wreath in birch bark-patterned paper ribbon.*

1 Bend one branch of the pine pick in the opposite direction to the other branch. Cut the stem off and bend the branches to follow the curve of the wreath bottom; glue in place. Glue two pomegranates side by side at the center of the pine bough and the other 3" to the left.

2 Glue the cones evenly spaced among the pine sprigs. Glue two apple slices on each side of the center pomegranates. Glue two apple slices 3" to the right of the pomegranates and one at each end of the pine.

3 Glue the peppers evenly spaced among the pine sprigs. Cut the juniper into 4" sprigs and glue evenly spaced, covering any area where the wreath shows through the pine.

4 Cut the barley into 4" sprigs and wire in clusters of three. Glue evenly spaced among the pine and juniper, extending in varied directions as shown. Cut the pepperberries into 3" sprigs and glue evenly spaced throughout the design. Turn the wreath so the arranged area is as shown in the large photo. Attach a wire loop hanger (see page 144) to the top back.

# FRUIT ARCH & CANDLE RINGS

by Anne-Marie Spencer

*one 28" long green PVC pine swag with pine cones*
*two 8" round green PVC pine candle rings*
*5 ½" yards of 1 ½" wide gold wire-edged organza ribbon*
*three 16" long latex fruit picks, each with one 2" long pear,*
*    one 2" wide apple, five various 1"–1 ½" fruits and many*
*    leaves*
*2 oz. of dried barley*
*two 4"x8" white pillar candles*
*24-gauge wire*
*low temperature glue gun and sticks*

1 **Swag:** Bend the swag into an arch as shown. Repeat with one fruit pick. Remove the center binding from a second fruit pick and separate into two pieces.

2 Glue the bent fruit pick to the swag center. Glue one half pick on each side so the last berry is at the end of the swag.

3 Cut two yards of ribbon and use it to make a puffy bow (see page 141) with a center loop, six 3" loops and 16" tails. Glue to the swag center; loop and glue a tail through the picks and greenery on each side. Cut the barley into 4" sprigs and set 12 aside for step 4. Wire the remaining sprigs into clusters of three and glue evenly spaced as shown.

4 **Candle rings:** Cut the third pick into separate fruits and leaves. Glue half equally spaced around each candle ring, leaving 4" open for a bow. Glue six barley sprigs evenly spaced around each ring. Cut four 4" ribbon lengths and set aside. Cut the remaining ribbon in half and use each to make a puffy bow with a center loop, six 3" loops and 10" tails. Glue one to each candle ring, looping and gluing the tails as for the swag. Shape each 4" length into a 2" loop. Glue two loops to each ring opposite the bow, 3" apart. Place a candle in the center of each ring.

# NATURAL
# CENTERPIECE

### by Anne-Marie Spencer

one 36" long green PVC pine centerpiece
2 stems of red latex poinsettias, each with one 7" wide blossom
2 red latex poinsettia picks, each with one 5" wide blossom and
    1 cluster of five ½" wide red berries
4 oz. of dried barley
6 oz. of green preserved boxwood
2 oz. of red preserved eucalyptus
2 oz. of dried brisa media
four 12" long cinnamon sticks
two 2¼"–3" wide dried lotus pods
four 3"–4" long pine cones
floral foam for drieds: one 3"x3"x2" block, two 1½" cubes
three ¾" wide green plastic candle cups on spikes
burgundy taper candles: two 10", one 12"
low temperature glue gun and sticks

1  Glue the large foam block to the center of the centerpiece. Cut the poinsettia
    stems to 2" and insert them side by side into the foam as shown. Glue a poinsettia pick into each end of the centerpiece.

2  Cut the eucalyptus and the boxwood into 6" sprigs and glue evenly spaced
    among the pine sprigs at similar angles. Glue a cinnamon stick into each corner of the foam, extending outward.

3  Cut the wheat into 5" sprigs and wire into clusters of five. Glue three clusters in
    a triangle on each side. Glue the cones as shown.

4  Glue a lotus pod near each central poinsettia. Cut the brisa media into 5" sprigs
    and glue evenly spaced throughout the design. Glue a 1½" foam cube 8" away from the center foam block on each side; insert one candle cup into the center of each foam block. Insert a candle into each cup.

# SANTA & ELVES CENTERPIECE

by Anne-Marie Spencer

one 36" green PVC pine
  centerpiece
one 15"x7" trellis arch on a
  moss-covered wood base
2 yards of 3" wide red
  metallic wired mesh ribbon
one 14" tall stuffed Santa Claus
two 8" tall stuffed elves
4 red latex poinsettia picks, each with one 4" wide blossom
  and 1 cluster of four ½" wide berries and leaves

2 holiday picks, each with a 1" square foil gift, 1" red ball,
  1 ½" long pine cone and cluster of ¼" wide red berries
6 gift picks, each with three ½" square foil-wrapped gifts
1 stem of white silk snowberries with 9 sprigs of many 1⁄16"
  wide berries
2 stems of red latex berries, each with thirteen 10"–15" long
  sprigs of many 1⁄8" wide berries
fourteen 1"–2" long pine cones
low temperature glue gun and sticks

1 Cut twelve 6"–8" sprigs from the centerpiece bottom.
  Glue the trellis to the centerpiece. Glue Santa's hands
and feet into the trellis. Glue the pine sprigs to the trellis
floor to cover the moss, angling them outward as shown.

2 Glue one red berry stem to each side, bending the
  sprigs to curve over the trellis as shown. Glue a
poinsettia on each side of the trellis and one on each
end of the centerpiece. Drape the ribbon as shown, gluing at each end.

3 Glue one elf sitting on the left side and one standing on the right, using a tendril from the trellis for
support. Glue a holiday pick to the front right trellis
and one to the left rear. Cut each gift pick stem to 2"
and glue the picks evenly spaced along the centerpiece
front and back.

4 Cut the snowberries into 2"–3" sprigs. Glue them
  and the cones evenly spaced throughout the design.

# SANTA WREATH

## by Anne-Marie Spencer

*one 10"x12" oval grapevine wreath with a woven lattice back*

*3⅔ yards of ⅝" wide red satin ribbon*

*1⅓ yard of ⅝" wide white satin ribbon*

*2 green PVC pine picks, each with twenty-six 5" long branches*

*one 7" tall stuffed Santa Claus with a bag of gifts*

*3 silk holiday picks, each with one 1½" apple and ball, three ¾"–1" long pine cones, eighteen ¼" wide berries and three 3" long pine sprigs*

*3 gift picks, each with three ½" gold gifts*

*eight 1½"–2" long gold pine cones*

*1 oz. of white glittered birch twigs*

*low temperature glue gun and sticks*

1 Cut all the 5" sprigs off the pine picks and glue them evenly spaced around the wreath, angled as shown by the arrows. Wrap 2⅓ yards of red ribbon spiral fashion around the greens, winding counterclockwise with wraps 5" apart.

2 Glue the Santa into the wreath center. Cut the balls off the holiday picks and set aside. Glue one pick to the wreath top and one on each side of Santa. Glue one ball 2" below the left pick, one 3" above the left pick and one between the top and right picks.

3 Glue one gift pick 2" above the left holiday pick, one 3" to the right of the top holiday pick and one just below the right holiday pick. Cut the twigs into 5" sprigs and glue evenly spaced angled as for the pine.

4 Glue the cones evenly spaced among the greenery. Cut a 1" red ribbon length and set aside. Hold the remaining ribbons together and handle as one to make a loopy bow (see page 140) with six 3" loops, a 5" tail and a 7" tail of each color. Wrap the center with the 1" length; glue to secure. Glue the bow to the wreath center bottom.

# HO HO HO BANNER

by Tracia Ledford

7"x23" natural canvas banner
7½" of ³⁄₁₆" wooden dowel
two 1½" round wooden doll heads
    with ³⁄₁₆" holes
24" of ⅜" wide red satin ribbon
one 1" wide white button
fabric paints: red, green, white, peach
red acrylic paint
white dimensional paint
black fine-tip permanent pen
#8 flat paintbrush
tracing paper, pencil, transfer paper
low temperature glue gun and sticks
    or tacky craft glue

1 Transfer (see page 143) the Santa pattern to the banner bottom. Paint his face peach and his hat red. Mix equal parts of peach and red to paint his cheeks and nose. Paint his eyes black. Paint his beard, mustache, eyebrows, hair and hat trim white; let dry. Outline with the pen. Use dimensional paint to squeeze a highlight dot on each cheek and eye. Squeeze a bumpy line on the eyebrows. Glue the button to the hat tip.

2 Transfer "HO" three times, angling the letters as shown. Paint them green or red as shown; let dry. Use the pen to draw stitch marks.

3 Paint the doll heads red; let dry. Insert the dowel through the top of the banner, then glue one ball onto each end. **Hanger:** Knot the ribbon around each end of the dowel, leaving 5" tails.

# SNOWMAN SWAG

by Anne-Marie Spencer

one 32" long green PVC pine swag with cones
2 ¼ yards of ¼" wide red bead garland
4 yards of 2 ½" wide red metallic PapeRibbon™
three 4" tall flocked snowmen with brooms
4 green silk holly picks, each with six 3" long leaves and 1
   cluster of six ¼" red berries
3 red gift picks, each with three ½" gifts
2 oz. of gold glittered preserved holly
3 oz. of white dried glittered German statice
low temperature glue gun and sticks

1 Fluff the branches on the swag and attach a wire loop hanger (see page 144) to the top back. Glue the snowmen as shown.

2 Glue one end of the beads to the top left of the swag back. Wrap it spiral fashion around the swag three times, gluing as needed to secure. Glue the holly picks as shown.

3 Glue a gift pick to the center top, one at the center left and one at the right bottom (see arrows). Use the ribbon to make an oblong bow (see page 140) with a center loop, two 3" loops, four 4" loops, six 5" loops, two 6" loops and 10" tails. Trim each tail in a V; glue the bow to the top center.

4 Cut the gold holly and statice into 4" sprigs and glue evenly spaced among the other materials.

# HOW TO DECORATE A TREE

## LIGHTS:

String the lights before adding ornaments; keep the lights on so you can check the effect as you work. Start at the top of the tree, winding downward in a zig-zag pattern. Weave the lights back and forth through the branches to give the tree depth and to hide the cord. Even if the tree is placed in a corner, be sure to string lights all the way around at the top, as most of the top of the tree is visible from different angles. Choose colors and styles which complement your other decorations. The more lights you use, the more brilliant your tree will be.

| LIGHTING NEEDS | |
|---|---|
| Tree Height | # of Mini Lights |
| 2 feet | 35–50 |
| 3 feet | 70–100 |
| 4 feet | 100–140 |
| 6 feet | 200–280 |
| 7 feet | 315–450 |
| 8 feet | 400–650 |
| 9 feet | 600–900 |
| 10 feet | 800–1100 |

| GARLAND NEEDS | |
|---|---|
| Tree Height | Garland Length |
| 2 feet | 15'–20' |
| 4 feet | 30'–40' |
| 6 feet | 50'–75' |
| 7 feet | 75'–95' |
| 9 feet | 125'–150' |

## GARLANDS

Draping garlands creates a symmetrical framework to highlight your tree and ornaments. Start at the bottom back of the tree and wire or twist one end of the garland around a branch tip. Drape it around the base and over the lower branches so that it hangs evenly and freely; move branch tips if necessary. If there is no branch tip where the garland should hang, wrap wire around it and hang it from a higher branch. Repeat for the succeeding rows, spacing them evenly. Trim the branch tips between the rows if necessary so they appear even. To join garlands, wire the ends together at the back of the tree. See the draping examples below.

For added elegance, tie shoestring bows (see page 141) of fabric or raffia to branch tips under the garlands, spacing them evenly. Ribbon or raffia strands also can be twisted around the garlands to match the bows. For extra sparkle, attach beads to the tops and bottoms of the garlands, or just to the tops.

## ORNAMENTS

For the best results, follow the color and design scheme set up by your lights and garlands. Place satin balls on inside branches, then add glass balls to both the inside and tips of the branches. Fill dark or empty spaces with glass balls. Try adding plain glass ornaments under the garland bows. Wire and hang three different solid-color balls together for a special touch. Hang large ornaments first, evenly spaced, then smaller items such as icicles and candy canes on the outer branches.

# Romantic

# Accents

An abundance of lace and ribbons distinguish these elegant pieces, designed to accent your home or become lovely gifts for the friend who loves frilly things. All the designs are beautiful, whether adorned with lots of lace and frills or just a touch.

The beautifully decorated Ribbon Rose Frame, page 28, establishes the romantic feeling of this section with buttons, roses, lace and ribbon added to a fabric frame. While being a bit Victorian in flavor, it will enhance any portrait, whether of an ancestor or a modern young girl.

Bottles and boxes are bedecked in ribbons, lace and pearls throughout these pages, creating some very special containers for gift items, or actually becoming the gifts. Try the Pin-Weaving boxes on page 41 and learn a new craft—it's so easy and the results are stunning gifts!

The Lacy Pink Hat on page 45 is a lovely accent for the bedroom or powder room wall. It is overflowing with lace and tulle and decorated with dried flowers. What a gorgeous gift!

All the pieces showcased here are wonderful and easily constructed, making your gift making and giving just that much faster and easier.

# Ribbon Rose Frame

by Kathy Thompson

one 5½"x7" ivory battenburg frame with an oval opening
brass charms: one 3½" long cherub, one ⅜" wide heart
ribbon roses: two ½" wide beige, five ⅜" wide beige, seven
    ½" wide ivory with green leaves
twelve ⅜"–⅝" wide buttons in assorted brown shades
½ yard of ⅛" wide ivory satin ribbon
eighteen 3mm iridescent pearls
woodtone spray stain, paper towels, acrylic spray sealer
low temperature glue gun and sticks or tacky craft glue

1   Seal the charms; let dry. Spray with stain; wipe off
    excess; let dry. Seal; let dry. Glue the cherub to the
lower left corner. Loop and glue the ribbon on each side
of the cherub around the frame opening as shown.

2   To the upper left, glue a cluster of two ivory roses, one
    ⅜" rose, two buttons and five pearls. To the lower
right, glue three buttons, three ivory roses, one ⅜" rose and
the heart charm. Glue the remaining roses, buttons and
pearls clustered along the outside of the cherub.

# Victorian Twig Easel

by Kathy Thompson

one 12"x4½" TWIGS™ easel
one 4"x6" old-fashioned postcard
two 3½" wide brass bow charms
fifteen ½" ivory ribbon roses with green leaves
small handful of green sheet moss
low temperature glue gun and sticks or tacky craft glue

1   Glue one charm to the center top of the
    postcard and the other upside down at the
bottom; let dry.

2   Glue a narrow strip of moss down each side of
    the postcard. Glue seven roses evenly spaced
into the moss on each side. Glue the last rose to
the center bottom of the upper charm. Glue or set
the postcard on the easel.

# Twig-Wrapped Birdhouse

### by LeNae Gerig

*3"x8" three-hole wooden birdhouse*
*3" round twig wreath*
*six ½"–¾" sprigs of dried pink pepperberries*
*½" long dried mini rosebuds: 5 yellow, 11 burgundy*
*ten 1"–1½" long sprigs of green preserved plumosus*
*two 1¼" long blue mushroom birds*
*handful of green sheet moss*
*acrylic paints: white, dark green*
*medium-grain sandpaper*
*#8 flat paintbrush*
*low temperature glue gun and sticks or tacky craft glue*

1 Leaving the wood rough and unsanded, paint the house sides and holes white. Paint the roof and perches green. Let dry.

2 Sand the edges and flat surfaces until some raw wood shows through.

3 Cut the binding from the wreath and pull it apart. Wrap it around the house from top to bottom, inserting the vine ends into holes as shown.

4 Glue ten moss tufts randomly spaced along the vines. Glue a plumosus sprig into each tuft. Cut the pepperberries into ½" clusters and glue 1–2 clusters into each tuft. Glue the rosebuds in clusters of 2–5, using larger clusters in tufts with fewer pepperberries; intersperse yellow buds among the burgundy buds. Glue a bird left of the lower hole and one to the upper right corner as shown in the large photo.

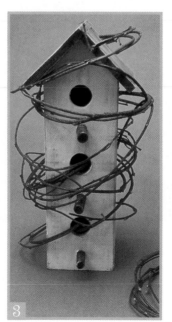

# Taffeta & Lace Pillow

by Marilyn Gossett

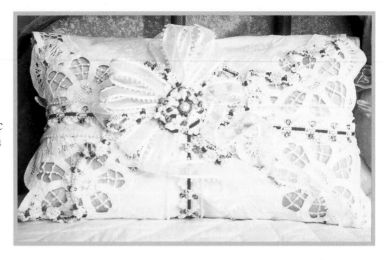

one 14"x20" white battenburg placemat
one 18"x30" piece of celadon green moiré taffeta fabric
1¾ yards of 1½" wide white organza pearl-edged ribbon
2 yards of ⅞" wide white organza/satin picot ribbon
40" of ½" wide white/red/green flat braid
one ½" round antique gold button with a pearl center
2 yards of ¾" wide white/red/green flat braid
polyester fiberfill, fabric glue
sewing machine or needle and thread

1  Press under ½" on each edge of the taffeta. Fold in
half crosswise, wrong sides together, and stitch or glue the seam, leaving a 3" opening. Stuff, then sew or glue the opening closed. Lay the placemat wrong side up and place the pillow crosswise in the center. Wrap the mat around the pillow, overlapping the short edges; sew or glue to secure. Wrap the 1½" ribbon lengthwise around the pillow. Trim excess and glue the ends at the center front. Repeat crosswise, then glue ¾" braid over the ribbon in both directions. Form the remaining 1½" ribbon into two loops, overlapping the ends. Wrap the center with thread; set aside for step 2.

2  Use the picot ribbon to make a puffy bow (see page 141) with eight 3" loops and 12" tails. Glue to the pillow center. Loop and glue the tails to the lower right as shown. Glue the ribbon loops from step 2 at the 9:00 and 12:00 positions. Cut four 4" lengths of ½" braid and glue the ends of each to form a loop. Glue the loops evenly spaced around the bow. Glue one end of a 12" length of ½" braid into the bow, loop and glue to the upper right corner. Repeat toward the lower left corner. Coil and glue the remaining 1" braid into a 1½" wide medallion, glue the button to the center and glue the medallion to the bow center.

# Daybed Sachet Pillow

by Marilyn Gossett

two 13" squares of pink/white striped chintz fabric
one 17"x13" piece of pink/ivory rose print fabric
one 6" white battenburg heart doily
1¾ yards of ¾" wide pink/yellow/green flat braid
½ yard of ½" wide pink/yellow/green flat braid
one 4½"x7" pink sachet packet
polyester fiberfill
sewing machine or needle and thread, fabric glue

1  **For the pillow:** Lay one square of striped fabric
right side up with the stripes running vertically. Fold the floral fabric in half crosswise, right sides out, and press. With the fold at the top, align the bottom and side edges with the striped fabric and sew ¼" from the raw edges to make a pocket. Sew 3¼" inside each side edge to create a small pocket on each side.

2  Glue ¾" trim across the pocket top, 1" below
the fold. Place the pillow squares right sides together, taking care that the stripes run the same direction. Sew in a ¼" seam, leaving a 4" opening. Clip the corners, turn right side out and stuff. Sew the opening closed. Glue the doily to the front of the pocket. Glue ½" trim around the edges. Glue ¾" trim around the pillow seam. Place the sachet in the center pocket.

# Rose-Trimmed Pillow

by LeNae Gerig

mauve moiré taffeta fabric: one 4"x20" piece, two 14"x20" pieces
19½"x13½" white battenburg placemat
10 oz. of polyester fiberfill
2 yards of 3" wide white organza ribbon
1½ yards of ⅜" wide mauve satin picot ribbon
½ yard of ⅝" wide light green satin ribbon
three ⅜" wide mauve ribbon roses with green leaves
1⅔ yards of ⅜" wide pink/green ribbon rose trim with green leaves
sewing machine or needle, white thread, straight pins, fabric glue

1  With right sides together, sew the 14"x20" fabric pieces together with a ¼" seam, leaving a 3" opening at one end. Turn right side out and press. Pin the placemat to the top of the pillow, marking the opening with pins.

2  Sew around the inside edge of the placemat trim, starting at one end of the opening and stopping at the other end. Stuff the pillow and sew the opening closed.

3  Glue the rose trim over the stitching. Use the white ribbon to make a loopy bow (see page 140) with six 3" loops, a 9" and an 18" tail. Glue the bow to the upper left of the placemat; loop and glue the tails as shown. Use the picot ribbon to make a loopy bow with six 2" loops, a 9" and an 18" tail. Glue diagonally to the center of the white bow. Loop and glue the tails over the white tails. Use the green ribbon to make a collar bow with 3" loops and 3" tails; glue diagonally to the picot bow.

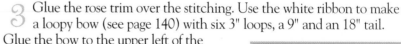

4  Fold the 4"x20" piece of fabric into a long tube with right sides together and sew a ¼" seam down the long side. Turn right side out and press to make a 1¾" wide ribbon. Follow the directions on page 141 to make a ribbon rose. Glue the rose to the bow center as shown in the large photo.

# Christmas Ball

by LeNae Gerig

one 5″ white Styrofoam® ball
15″ square of light pink tulle
4⅔ yards of 1″ wide ivory double-faced satin
   ribbon
1½ yards of ¼″ wide dusty rose satin ribbon
1½ yards of ¼″ wide dusty rose/green rose braid
3 yards of ½″ wide dusty rose/gold flat braid
1½ yards of 4mm ivory fused pearls
one 3½″ long ivory tassel
one ¾″ wide ivory satin rose
24-gauge wire
low temperature glue gun and sticks or tacky craft
   glue

1  Place the ball in the center of the tulle, gather it around the sides and secure at the top with wire. Trim the excess tulle. Wrap 17″ of ivory ribbon around the ball, securing with tacky glue. Repeat with two more 17″ lengths, dividing the ball into six sections.

2  Glue rose/green braid to the center of each ribbon length. Cut twelve 17″ lengths of rose/gold braid and glue one along each side of each ribbon length. Cut the pearls into six 9″ lengths and glue evenly spaced between the ribbon lengths.

3  Use 1⅔ yards of ivory ribbon to make a puffy bow (see page 141) with twelve 2½″ loops and no tails. Glue to the top of the ball. Use the rose ribbon to make a puffy bow with a 10″ center loop (for the hanger) and eight 2″ loops. Glue to the center of the ivory bow. Glue the ribbon rose to the center of the rose bow.

4  Use the remaining ivory ribbon to make a puffy bow with twelve 2″ loops and no tails. Glue to the bottom of the ball. Cut the hanger from the tassel and glue the tassel to the center of the bow.

# Doily Ball
by LeNae Gerig

one 4" Styrofoam® ball
one 12" wide ivory crocheted doily with scallops
1 yard of ½" wide mauve gimp braid
½ yard of ⅜" wide ivory flat lace
30" of 3mm ivory fused pearls
2 yards of ⅜" wide mauve satin ribbon
four ⅜" wide ivory ribbon roses with green
   leaves
22-gauge wire
low temperature glue gun and sticks or tacky
   craft glue

1   Place the ball in the doily center. Gather the edges around the ball and wire tightly at the bottom.

2   Cut the trim into three 12" lengths; glue the end of one length close to the wire, wrap it around the ball and glue the other end. Repeat with the other lengths, dividing the ball into six sections.

3   (See the large photo.) Cut the pearls into six 5" lengths and glue one in the center of each section. Use the ribbon to make a loopy bow (see page 140) with a 7" center loop (the hanger), fourteen 2" loops and no tails. Glue the bow to the center top of the ball.

4   Use the lace to make a loopy bow with a center loop, six 1½" loops and no tails; glue to the center of the first bow. Glue three ribbon roses evenly spaced around the ball below the bow loops and one at the center bottom.

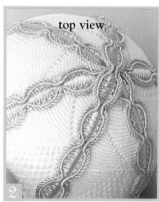

# Tricycle with Roses

by Kathy Thompson

*one 9"x7" black wire/wood tricycle*
*1 yard of ¼" wide lavender satin picot ribbon*
*ribbon roses: four 1" wide purple, three ⅜" wide purple, five ⅝" wide lavender*
*six ⅜" wide white silk rosebuds*
*nine ⅝" wide pink silk daisies*
*¼ oz. of white dried baby's breath*
*⅛ oz. of green preserved plumosus*
*22-gauge wire*
*low temperature glue gun and sticks or tacky craft glue*

1   Use the ribbon to make a loopy bow (see page 140) with six 1½" loops and 4½" tails. Glue it at the base of the handlebars with the tails extending down and crossing at the wheel center.

2   Cut the baby's breath and plumosus into ¾"–2" sprigs. Glue the shortest sprig of each at the tail crossing. Glue three sprigs of each extending outward from the bow center. Set a few sprigs aside for step 4; glue the rest evenly spaced between the back wheels.

3   Glue a ⅜" ribbon rose at the tail crossing. Glue a 1" ribbon rose to the bow center with a ⅝" ribbon rose above right of it. Glue three 1" ribbon roses evenly spaced between the back wheels. Glue a ⅜" ribbon rose 1" away on each side of the center rose. Glue the remaining ⅝" ribbon roses in a square around the center rose.

4   Glue a white rosebud above and one below the ribbon roses on the handlebars. Glue three daisies evenly spaced among the roses and buds. Glue the remaining white rosebuds evenly spaced around the center rose of the lower arrangement. Glue six daisies evenly spaced among the roses. Glue the remaining plumosus and baby's breath to fill any empty spaces.

# Grandmother's Doll

### by LeNae Gerig

3½" long plastic doll head with two 1¾" long
   arms
unbleached muslin fabric: one 15"x45" piece,
   two 4"x4" pieces
15"x54" piece of ivory tulle fabric
round ivory battenburg doilies: one 6" wide, one
   10" wide
1½ yards of 1" wide ivory crocheted lace
1⅔ yards of ¾" wide ivory flower appliqué trim
⅓ yard of 1" wide ivory satin ribbon
⅞ yard of ⅛" wide ivory satin ribbon
4" of 4mm ivory fused pearls
⅝" wide gold heart charm
handful of polyester fiberfill
needle, ivory thread
2 cups of warm black coffee
large bowl
fabric glue

actual height 17"

1. Place the fabric and coffee in the bowl to
   soak for 5–10 minutes. Wring out excess
coffee and lay the fabric out to dry; do not
iron out the wrinkles. Glue a ¼" hem along
one 45" edge of the large muslin piece. Glue lace to
extend from under the hem. Glue flower trim above the
lace as shown. Save 2" of trim for step 4.

2. Sew a running stitch ⅛" from one 54" edge of the
   tulle and gather to fit around the doll shoulders;
glue in place. Repeat with the lace-edged muslin, gluing
it over the tulle. Glue the fabric edges together in back.

3. **Sleeves:** Fold each 4" muslin square in half and
   sew the edges together to form a tube. Turn right
side out, sew a running stitch ⅛" from one end and pull
to gather. Lightly stuff with fiberfill. Glue a 4" lace
length around the sleeve 1½" from the ungathered end.
Wrap a 9" length of ⅛" ribbon above the lace to form
an elbow; tie in a shoestring bow (see page 141) with
½" loops and ½" tails. Repeat below the lace to form a
cuff. Glue the gathered ends of the sleeves to the doll
shoulders. Glue an arm into each cuff so 1⅜" extends—
be careful to position the hands with the palms facing.

4. **Apron:** Pleat one scallop of the 8" doily and glue
   to the center back of the 1" ribbon. Glue the
remaining 2" of flower trim to the ribbon center front.
Tie around the doll's waist in a shoestring bow with
1½" loops and 1½" tails. **Collar:** Cut the 6" doily from
a corner to the center, wrap around her neck and glue
the back closed. Glue the pearls around her neck. With
the remaining ⅛" ribbon, make a shoestring bow with
⅜" loops and tails. Glue the bow and charm to the
collar front as shown in the large photo.

back view

actual height 13"

# Porcelain Angel Tree Topper

by LeNae Gerig

2¼ yards of white border eyelet fabric
   with a scalloped edge
10" tall clear plastic cone
3½" tall porcelain doll head with 2"
   long arms
2 yards of 9" wide white tulle
3⅓ yards of ¼" wide burgundy rose
   braid with ¼" loops on one side
2½ yards of ¼" wide flat gold braid
   with ¼" loops
8" square white battenburg doily
5" round white battenburg doily
one ¾" wide burgundy ribbon rose
12" of ⅛" wide burgundy satin ribbon
1½ yards of ½" wide burgundy satin
   picot ribbon
needle, white thread, 24-gauge wire
low temperature glue gun and sticks or
   tacky craft glue

**3** **Collar:** Cut the 5" doily to the center, then cut a ½" X in the center. Tuck the raw edges under, wrap around her neck and glue at the back. Glue gold braid to the neck edge of the collar, along the inner edge of the lace trim, and around her head for a halo. Glue the rose to the center front as shown.

**4** **Wings:** Glue rose braid around the inner edge of the lace trim on the square doily. Turn over and repeat on the other side. Pinch the center of the doily, wire to secure and glue to the angel's back. Use the picot ribbon to make an oblong bow (see page 140) with a center loop, six 2"–2½" loops and 12" tails. Glue the bow over the wired area of the wings. Glue the remaining gold trim to the skirt hem and the remaining rose braid ½" above it.

**1** Glue the head to the top of the cone. Sew a running stitch ¼" from one long edge of the tulle, pull to gather and glue to the cone just under the doll's chest. Cut 10" off the border edge of the eyelet. Cut two 4"x4½" pieces from the scalloped edge, placing a 4" edge along the scallops, and set aside for step 2. Gather the remaining fabric as for the tulle, spreading the gathers around the cone and gluing to secure. Glue the back edges of the skirt together.

**2** Fold a 4"x4½" piece lengthwise, right sides together, and sew along the 4½" edges in a ¼" seam. Turn right side out; glue a hand into the scalloped end. Tie the wrist with a 6" length of ⅛" ribbon, making a shoestring bow (see page 141) with ½" loops and ¾" tails. Pinch the open end together and glue under the angel's shoulder. Repeat for the other sleeve.

back view

# Ribbon Roses Potpourri Basket

by Kathy Thompson

*one 7" wide brown willow heart basket
with a 5" handle*
*1 yard of 3¾" wide dark green grosgrain
ribbon with gold wired edges*
*20" of 4mm ivory fused pearls*
*9" of 10mm ivory fused pearls*
*one 10" round ivory crocheted pineapple
doily*
*ribbon roses: sixteen 1" wide burgundy
ruffled, fifteen ½" wide ivory*
*1 oz. of burgundy dried rosebuds*
*2 oz. of rose potpourri*
*needle, dark green thread*
*low temperature glue gun and sticks or
tacky craft glue*

side view

*1* Cut the ribbon into two 18"
lengths. Sew a running stitch
along the center of each and gather to
fit around one side of the basket rim;
glue. Cut the 4mm pearls into ten 2"
lengths; glue the ends to form ten
loops.

*2* Cut the 3½" center circle from
the doily; glue it over the handle
center. Glue two pearl loops end to
end at the center, a 1" rose on each

side of the handle top and a ½" rose on each side of the 1" roses over
the points of the pearl loops.

*3* Cut two 2-scallop and four 1-scallop sections from the remaining
doily. Glue a 2-scallop section at each handle base. Glue three 1"
roses, two ½" roses and two pearl loops to each 2-scallop section. Glue
two 1-scallop sections evenly spaced on each side of the rim. Glue two
1" roses, one ½" rose and one bead loop to each 1-scallop section.

*4* Glue the remaining ½" roses evenly spaced along the ribbon center between the scallop sections. Cut the 10mm pearls apart. Fill
the basket with the potpourri, dried rosebuds and pearls.

# Potpourri Heart by LeNae Gerig

*one 5" wide white battenburg heart sachet with a ribbon
hanger and 1" opening for filling*
*⅛ cup scented potpourri*
*⅓ yard of ¼" wide burgundy/gold rose braid*
*three ⅝" wide burgundy ribbon roses with green leaves*
*four ⅜" wide white ribbon roses with green leaves*
*brass charms: one ⅝" snowflake, one ¾" long key, one
¾" wide heart*
*five ½" long sprigs of white dried baby's breath*
*low temperature glue gun and sticks or tacky craft glue*

Fill the heart with potpourri and glue the opening
closed. Glue the braid to the inside edge of the
sachet lace. Glue the ribbon roses, charms and baby's
breath as shown.

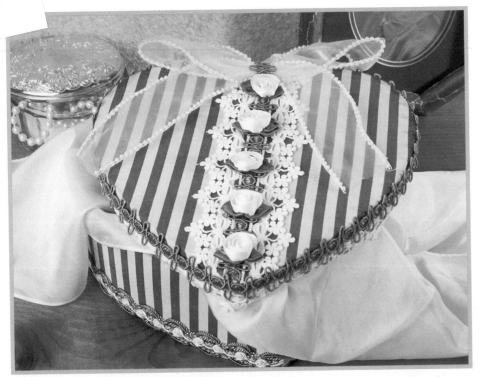

½ yard of blue/white striped chintz fabric
8"x3"x8" papier-mâché heart box
1 yard of ¾" wide blue flat loopy braid
42" of 1" wide white appliqué trim with one straight and one
    scalloped edge
26" of 1" wide blue/white rose braid with scalloped edges
five 1" wide white ribbon roses
24" of 1½" wide pearl-edged organza ribbon
tacky craft glue, sponge brush, paper plate
    (or spray adhesive)

1 Lay the lid on the wrong side of a 9" fabric square,
   positioning it so the stripes run vertically. Trace
around the lid ; cut out 1" outside the line. Squeeze a 3"
puddle of craft glue onto a paper plate. Use the sponge
brush to apply glue to the top and sides, then smooth the
fabric onto the lid and over the edges, pressing out any
bubbles or wrinkles. Repeat to cover the box bottom.

2 Cut a 25"x2½" fabric strip with crosswise stripes.
   Apply glue to the box sides, stopping ½" below the
top edge. Smooth the fabric onto the box sides. Glue
the blue/white braid around the bottom edge.

3 Glue white trim around the lower edge of the lid,
   positioning it so the scallops extend below the lid
edge. Glue loopy braid along the top edge so the lower
loops overlap the straight edge of the white trim.

4 Glue two rows of white trim ⅜" apart to the center
   of the box lid as shown in the large photo, scallops
to the outside. Glue loopy braid between the edges of
the white—the loops will overlap on both sides. Use
the ribbon to make a collar bow (see page 140) with 3"
loops and 4½"–5" tails. Wrap a 2" piece of loopy braid
around the bow center; glue to secure. Trim the tails
diagonally and glue the bow to the lid as shown.

# Two Bottles
## by LeNae Gerig

**for the mauve bottle:**
13" tall green glass bottle with cork
7 yards of ¼" wide mauve satin braid
1 yard of 1½" wide mauve taffeta
   ribbon with gold wired edges
2 yards of ¾" wide ivory flat lace
1¾" long gold heart charm
tacky craft glue

**for the gold bottle:**
7½" tall green glass bottle with cork
12" of 4" wide ivory scalloped flat lace
½ yard of ¼" wide ivory braid
1 yard of ⅜" wide metallic gold
   grosgrain picot ribbon
gold spray webbing
spray acrylic sealer
metallic gold acrylic paint, #6 flat brush
three 1" wide ivory silk rosebuds
¼ oz. of white dried German statice
¾" wide heart charm
needle, ivory thread
low temperature glue gun and sticks or
   tacky craft glue

1 **Mauve bottle:** Apply glue to the bottle center and wrap the braid tightly spiral-fashion around it. Glue the charm to the center front of the braid—this will be the front of the bottle.

2 Use the lace to make a loopy bow (see page 140) with twelve 2½" long loops and one 5" tail. Glue the bow to the base of the neck. Wrap the tail around the neck and glue behind the bow. Use the mauve ribbon to make a puffy bow with a center loop, four 1¾" loops and 6" tails. Glue diagonally to the lace bow center. Ripple the tails as shown.

3 **Gold bottle:** Spray the bottle with sealer and let dry. Spray the bottle with webbing, paint the cork gold, and let dry. Seal. Sew a running stitch along one long edge of the lace and gather around the bottle neck, gluing to secure. Use the braid to make a collar bow (see page 140) with 2" loops and 5" tails. Glue to the front bottle neck. Knot the tails 1½" from the ends.

4 Use the gold ribbon to make a loopy bow with four 1½" loops and 5" tails; wire the remaining ribbon into the bow for another set of tails. Glue to the center of the braid bow. Glue the rosebuds in a triangle to the bow center. Glue 1"–2½" statice sprigs around the buds; glue the heart charm at the lower right.

1 ⅝" wide satin ribbon poinsettias with pearl centers:
   1 white, 2 ivory
nine ¾" long green silk rose leaves
two ⅜" wide ivory satin ribbon roses with green leaves
⅔ yard of ⅞" wide ivory flat lace
⅓ yard of ⅜" wide ivory satin ribbon
3" of ⅝" wide ivory satin ribbon
1 yard of ⅛" wide white satin ribbon
1 yard of ⅛" wide ivory satin ribbon
⅔ yard of white 4mm fused pearls
30-gauge wire, wire cutters
low temperature glue gun and sticks or tacky craft glue

1  **Lace rosettes:** Cut three 6" wire lengths and three 9" lace lengths. Thread a wire in and out along the straight edge of each lace length, gather the lace on the wire and twist the wire ends together to secure.

2  Glue a poinsettia to the center of each rosette and three leaves evenly spaced around each poinsettia.

3  Turn under 1½" on each end of the ⅜" ribbon and glue to secure. Glue the white poinsettia to the center of the ribbon with an ivory poinsettia ¼" away on each side. Cut each ⅛" ribbon in half, hold a length of each color together and tie a shoestring bow (see page 141) with ¾" loops and 6"–6½" tails. Repeat. Glue the bows between the poinsettias as shown.

4  Cut the ⅝" ribbon into three 1" lengths and glue one over the center back of each lace circle to anchor it to the ribbon. Glue a 6½" and a 5½" pearl length to the center of each bow as shown in the large photo above. Glue a ribbon rose to the bow center.

back view

# Pin-Weaving Boxes

### by Marilyn Gossett

2 yards of 6" wide pink tulle
steam iron, damp pressing cloth
straight pins, safety pins
acrylic paints: white, lavender, aqua
1" sponge brush, 1" square of household sponge
9" square of foam board or corrugated cardboard
tacky craft glue

**for the large box:**
7½"x3"x7½" papier-mâché heart box
8" square of paper-backed fusible web
1⅓ yards each of the following trims:
* ½" wide aqua/white flat braid
* ½" wide lavender/white flat braid
* ⅜" wide aqua loopy braid
* ⅜" wide lavender loopy braid
* ⅜" wide white satin picot ribbon
* ¼" wide aqua satin picot ribbon
* ¼" wide ivory/metallic gold rose braid
¾ yard of ½" wide aqua/white flat braid (box trim)
¾ yard of ⅜" wide lavender loopy braid (lid edging)

**for the small box:**
6"x2½"x5½" papier-mâché heart box
7" square of paper-backed fusible web
1 yard each of the following trims:
* ⅜" wide white satin picot ribbon
* ¼" wide aqua satin picot ribbon
* ¼" wide ivory/metallic gold rose braid
* ½" wide lavender/white flat braid
½ yard each of the following trims:
* ½" wide aqua/white flat braid
* ⅜" wide aqua loopy braid
⅝ yard of ½" wide lavender/white flat braid (box trim)
⅝ yard of ⅜" wide aqua loopy braid (lid edging)

1 (Refer to the large photo.) **Box:** Paint the large box lavender, inside and out. Paint the small box aqua. Let dry. Dip the sponge square in white paint and dab it evenly over each box and lid, letting the base color show through. Repeat with aqua on the lavender box and lavender on the aqua box. Let dry. Glue the box trim around each box ¼" above the lower edge.

2 **Large pin-weaving:** Set aside the lid edging. Cut the remaining trims into 8" lengths. Lay the web on the center of the foam board, paper side down. Lay the trims on the web in this order: aqua loopy, lavender loopy, aqua/white, lavender white. Repeat until these trims are all placed. Space the rows evenly and secure with a straight pin in each end—angle all the pins outward to keep them out of the way of the iron. Keep the rows parallel.

3 For the vertical rows, use the three remaining trims in this order: white ribbon, aqua ribbon, white/gold braid. Pin one end of the first trim at the top. Attach a safety pin to the other end and weave it over the first horizontal row, under the second; continue to the end and secure with a straight pin. Repeat until all the trims are used. Lay the pressing cloth over the weaving and press the trims onto the web—refer to the manufacturer's instructions for time and temperature, as brands vary. Let cool; remove the pins and paper backing.

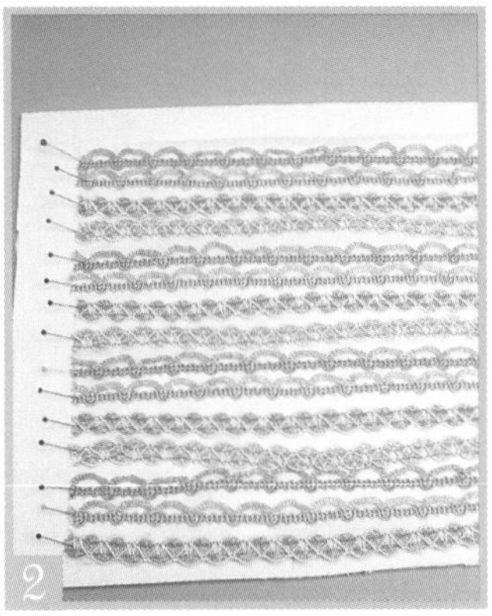

4 (Refer to the large photo.) **Small pin-weaving:** Follow steps 2–3, but cut the trims into 6" lengths. Follow this order for the horizontal trims: white ribbon, white/gold braid, aqua ribbon. Follow this order for the vertical trims: lavender/white, aqua loopy, lavender/white, aqua/white. **Finishing:** Lay the box lid on the square, trace and cut out. Glue to the top of the lid, then glue the edging to hide the cut edge. Stack the boxes as shown and tie with the tulle, making a shoestring bow (see page 140) with 4" loops and 8" tails.

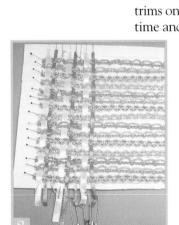

by Marilyn Gossett

*round papier-mâché boxes: one 4½"x1½", one 5½"x2½"*
*white round battenburg doilies: one 3", one 5"*
*white round crocheted doilies: one 4", one 5"*
*1¾ yards of ¼" wide red rose braid*
*⅞ yard of ¼" wide white heart appliqué trim*
*½ yard of 1" wide white heart appliqué trim*
*ribbon roses: three 1" wide red ruffled, seven ¾" white*
*1 yard of 6" wide white tulle*
*acrylic paints: white, ivory, metallic gold*
*1" sponge brush, 1" square of household sponge*
*low temperature glue gun and sticks or tacky craft glue*

1 Paint the boxes and lids white, inside and out; let dry. Dip the sponge square in ivory paint and dab it lightly over the white. Repeat with gold, letting the base color show through.

2 Glue rose braid around the top of each lid and the bottom of the large box. Glue 1" trim below the braid on the large box. Glue ¼" heart trim below the braid on the small box and halfway between the 1" trim and the lower braid on the large box.

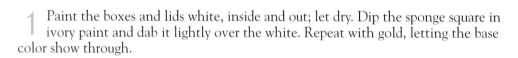

3 Glue the 3" doily to the small box lid. Glue the 5" doily to the front of the large box lid, then glue the small box to the back of the lid as shown. Pinch each crocheted doily in the center and wrap with thread to secure. Glue the 4" doily to the top left of the small box and the 5" doily to the front center of the large lid where it joins the small box.

top view

4 Glue two red and four white roses to the top of the small box. Glue one red and two white roses to the large box. Glue the last white rose to the front of the small box lid above the lower red rose. Cut the remaining rose braid into three 3" and three 2" lengths. Fold each into a loop and glue the ends. Glue a 1½" loop into the back of the top cluster and two, angling outward, into the front of the lower cluster. Glue a 1" loop into the back of the lower cluster and two, angling outward, into the front of the upper cluster. Wrap the tulle around the boxes and tie at the top back, making a shoestring bow (see page 141) with 3½" loops and 3½" tails, as shown in the large photo above.

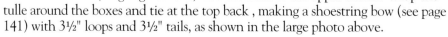

# Abaca Angel
## by Marilyn Gossett

one 9" tall abaca angel
2 yards of 8" wide ivory flat lace
3 yards of 2" wide ivory gathered lace
2 yards of burgundy/metallic gold rose braid
⅔ yard of ⅝" wide white loop appliqué trim
one ½" wide burgundy ribbon rose
small handful of auburn Mini Curl™ hair
small handful of green sheet moss
twenty-four ½" long burgundy dried rosebuds
ten ½" long sprigs of white dried statice sinuata
needle, ivory thread
pink powdered blush, cotton swab
low temperature glue gun and sticks or tacky craft glue

1  Remove the ponytail and wings from the angel; separate the hands. **Bodice:** Cut a 4" length of flat lace and fold in thirds to 1⅓"x8". Drape around the angel's neck, crossing and gluing the ends in front. Wrap and glue a 4" length of rose braid over the center of the lace. **Skirt:** Sew a running stitch 1" below one long edge of the remaining flat lace. Pull to gather and glue around the angel's waist. Glue the seam closed in the back. Glue rose braid around the waist. **Skirt rosettes:** Cut five 3" lengths of rose braid. Coil each into a flat spiral 1" across. Glue evenly spaced across the skirt front, 2" above the lower edge.

2  Cut the hair into 4" lengths. Starting at the center back bottom of the head and working to the top front, glue the centers of the lengths in rows. Fluff the hair, pull it up into a topknot and secure with a 5" length of loop trim. Glue small moss tufts along the front of the trim; glue five dried rosebuds evenly spaced into the moss. Glue the ribbon rose to the bodice opening. Blush her cheeks.

3  **Garland:** Measure 5" from one end of the remaining loop trim and glue into one hand. Repeat on the other side, forming a draped loop between her hands. Cut a 13" length of rose braid and glue over the loop trim, making 2½" tails. Glue a 1" ball of moss to each hand. Glue a moss tuft to the center of each loop trim tail, attaching it to her skirt. Glue a 5" band of moss to the center of the loop garland. Glue two rosebuds and a statice sprig into each moss tuft. Glue the remaining rosebuds and statice evenly spaced into the garland moss.

4  **Wings:** Sew a running stitch along the bound edge of the gathered lace and gather it to fit around the wings as shown; glue to secure. Glue rose braid to the front edge of the wings as shown in the large photo. Glue the wings to her back.

back view

actual height 10"

# Heart Sachet Angel

by Marilyn Gossett

two 4" wide white battenburg heart doilies
white square battenburg doilies: one 6", one 8"
⅛ cup of potpourri
small handful of polyester fiberfill
⅔ yards of ⅜" wide white picot satin ribbon
15" of 4mm white fused pearls
1 yard of ⅛" wide mauve satin ribbon
1 yard of ⅛" wide white satin ribbon
one 1½" wide wooden ball
four ⅜" wide mauve ribbon roses with green
   leaves
small handful of strawberry blond Mini Curl™ hair
black fine-tip permanent pen
acrylic paints: pale peach, pink
paintbrushes: #6 flat, #1 liner
pink powdered blush, cotton swab
needle, white thread, 30-gauge wire
tracing paper, transfer paper, pencil
low temperature glue gun and sticks or tacky
   craft glue

1 **Body:** Glue the hearts wrong sides together, leaving a 1" opening. Stuff with fiberfill and potpourri, then glue the opening closed. Cut 9" of picot ribbon and knot ½" from each end. Glue the ribbon center to the heart back and bring the knots to the front for hands.

2 **Skirt:** Sew a running stitch ¼" from one edge of the 8" doily and gather to 2" wide. **Wings:** Pinch the center of the 6" doily and wire to secure.

3 Glue the skirt to the body bottom, the wings to the top back and the hands to the front. Cross the ends of the remaining picot ribbon, leaving 1" tails, and glue to the front for a hanger. Paint the ball peach; let dry. Transfer (see page 143) the face and go over the lines with the pen. Use the liner to paint the mouth pink. Blush the cheeks. Glue the head to the crossed area of the hanger.

4 Cut the hair into 2"–4" lengths. Starting at the center back bottom of the head and working to the top front, glue the centers of the lengths in rows. Fluff the hair, glue to secure it at the sides of the head, and trim the front to ½" for bangs. Cut a 3" pearl length, glue the ends together and glue for a halo. Hold the ⅛" ribbons together to make a loopy bow (see page 140) with four 1¼" loops and 7" tails. Glue the bow into her hands as shown in the large photo. Glue the center of the remaining pearls and three ribbon roses to the bow center. Glue the last rose to the left of the halo.

# Lacy Pink Hat

### by Marilyn Gossett

one 9½" wide straw hat
1 yard of ⅜" wide pink/white flat braid
1⅞ yards of ⅜" wide pink rose braid
2 yards of ⅝" wide pink organza ribbon
2 yards of 6" wide pink tulle
3 yards of 2" wide ivory gathered lace
1¼ yards of 2" wide ivory flat lace
twenty-one ½" wide dried pink rosebuds
1 oz. of white dried baby's breath
1 oz. of green sheet moss
ivory acrylic spray paint, newspapers
24-gauge wire, one U-shaped floral pin
low temperature glue gun and sticks or
    tacky craft glue

1 Spread out newspapers and spray the hat ivory; let dry. Cut 12" of rose braid and glue in a circle around the top of the hat crown (see arrow). Glue two rows of gathered lace around the outer edge of the brim, 1" apart, beginning and ending both rows in the same place. Cut 12" of rose braid and glue to the bottom of the brim, centered on the lace seams. Fold the edge up and glue to the crown as shown.

2 Cut 24" of organza ribbon and set aside for step 4. Loop and glue the remaining ribbon over the bound edge of the second row of lace. Loop and glue rose braid over the ribbon as shown.

3 Glue a 1" band of moss around the base of the crown. Glue 20 dried rose buds evenly spaced into the moss; glue 1" sprigs of baby's breath among the roses.

4 Cut the tulle into two 1-yard lengths. Hold together to tie a shoestring bow (see page 141) with 6" loops and 14" tails. Glue the bow to the folded brim of the hat. Use the flat lace to tie a loopy bow (see page 140) with two 4" loops and 14" tails; glue to the tulle bow center. Knot the center of the remaining organza ribbon and glue the knot to the center of the lace bow. Use the remaining rose braid to make a loopy bow with two 4" loops and no tails. Glue it to the bow center. Glue the center of the pink/white braid into the bow center. Glue a 1½" tuft of moss, the remaining rosebuds and the remaining baby's breath just above the bow centers. Glue the U-pin to the top back for a hanger.

# Quick & Easy Gifts

Creating Christmas gifts for friends and relatives provides a warm and special feeling during the holidays—especially if the gifts are quick and easy to make! We've included many projects to be used to dress up romantic corners of a room, adding romance and elegance. The golden touches on the candle, picture frame and tray, shown here, lend a richness to the dresser while being practical and pretty accents.

The eucalyptus corner swag enhances a picture and frame, adding both style and warmth to the room. The decorated container of potpourri began its life as a terra cotta pot; it's now a lovely accent to this bedroom, providing the delightful scent and texture of potpourri.

What little girl wouldn't be delighted with the ribbon-wrapped headband adorned with roses, also made from ribbons? A splendid gift to greet her on Christmas morning—and so easy to make!

Many charming and sweet gifts can be found within these pages. A cute angel, a cheerful bear and a clever slate make perfect gifts for that favorite teacher. Simple painting techniques enhance a candle, a saucer and two clever t-shirts—it's all in the dots!

Whatever your needs are for gifts this Christmas, the ideas found here will make your season shine. From the delightful to the stunning—and all so quick and easy!

# Eucalyptus Napkin Ring Swag

by Karin Hupp

*1 blue/white plaid ceramic napkin ring*
*1 stem of pink silk petunias with six 1"–1½" blossoms and many leaves*
*1 stem of white silk baby's breath with 6 sprigs, each with a 1"–1½" wide cluster of ½" blossoms*
*2 oz. of dark green preserved eucalyptus*
*6" of 20-gauge wire*
*low temperature glue gun and sticks or tacky craft glue*

**1** Form two equal bunches of eucalyptus, each containing 8–10 stems 4"–10" long. Glue one into each side of the napkin ring. Set the remaining eucalyptus aside for step 4.

**2** Cut the petunias into six 4"–6" sprigs, each with a blossom and several leaves. Glue three into each side of the napkin ring extending so the blossoms form a triangle.

**3** Cut the baby's breath sprigs off the stem and glue three evenly spaced among the petunias on each side.

**4** Glue the remaining eucalyptus among the flowers to fill any empty spaces. On the back, twist one end of the wire around the base of a eucalyptus branch on each side of the napkin ring to form a hanger.

# Eucalyptus Frame

## by Karin Hupp

8"x10" mahogany-stained wooden frame
1 stem of burgundy latex stromia with
   three 2" wide blossoms, a bud and
   variegated leaves
1 stem of blue latex berries with nine
   4"–9" sprigs, each with a curly stem
   and a 2" long cluster of 1/8" wide
   berries
4 oz. of green lacquered preserved
   eucalyptus (twenty-four 3"–10"
   stems)
2"x2"x1" block of floral foam for silks
   and drieds
small handful of Spanish moss
low temperature glue gun and sticks or
   tacky craft glue

**1** Glue the foam to the top right corner of the frame. Glue moss to cover the foam.

**2** Glue the eucalyptus into the foam, placing the longest stems to extend along the frame sides and shorter stems evenly spaced as shown.

**3** Cut the stromia blossoms and bud with 2" stems. Glue the bud extending downward along the right side of the frame. Glue the blossoms evenly spaced arching across the corner.

**4** Cut the berry sprigs off the main stem. Glue evenly spaced among eucalyptus sprigs of similar lengths.

actual height 6"

# Teacher Angel
## by Marilyn Gossett

one 1¼" round wooden head bead
one 3½" long wooden doll pin with stand
four 2" long wooden teardrops (wings)
one 2"x¼" wooden heart (feet)
one 1"x1"x½" wooden book
green print fabric: one 5"x10" rectangle
    (body), one 3"x8" rectangle (arms), one
    1"x8" strip (bow)
acrylic paints: pale peach, white, black, brown
white paint marker
fine-tip black permanent pen
paintbrushes: #4 flat, #0 liner
satin acrylic sealer
auburn Mini Curl ™ doll hair
⅝" wide buttons: 1 gold/black flower, 1 gold
    apple,1 red apple
one ⅜" wide black heart button
one ¾" wide "gold" wedding ring
12" of jute twine
polyester fiberfill, needle, green thread
tracing paper, pencil
low temperature glue gun and sticks or tacky
    craft glue

**1** Glue the head to the doll pin and the pin to the stand. Glue the stand to the heart as shown. Glue the teardrops together as shown for wings. Paint the wings black. Paint the upper body peach. Paint the stand, heart base and book brown. Dip dot (see page 143) black eyes. Use the black pen to draw the nose and mouth. Blush the cheeks, then dip dot white highlights. Seal all the painted pieces. Use the white paint marker to write on the wings as shown.

**2** **Dress:** Sew a running stitch along each long edge of the largest fabric piece. Pull to gather it around the neck and base; secure with glue. Stuff fiberfill through the back seam to fill the body. Sew a running stitch around the waist area, pull to gather it slightly and knot the ends in the back. **Bow:** Use the smallest fabric strip to tie a shoestring bow (see page 141) with 1" loops and 1½"–2" tails. Glue to her right waist.

**3** **Arms:** Fold the rectangle in thirds; glue the raw edge down. Knot the center for hands and glue the ends to the top back. Glue the red apple button to her hands and the gold apple button to the bow center. Glue the wings to her back.

**4** Fluff the hair and glue to her head. Glue the flower button to the left side and the wedding ring for a halo. Wrap the book with twine as you would wrap a gift. Knot close to the book, then slip one end behind her arm and knot the ends together. Glue the heart button under her chin as shown in the large photo.

top view

# Teacher Bear

### by Marilyn Gossett

one 9" tall jointed plush bear
one 3" square slate
one 1" long chalk eraser
one 1½" piece of ³⁄₁₆" wooden dowel
two ⅝" round red buttons
6" of jute twine
one ½" wide red plastic apple button
one ½"x24" strip of green/cream plaid fabric
pink powdered blush, cotton swab
white acrylic paint, #2 flat paintbrush
white paint marker
low temperature glue gun and sticks or tacky craft glue

**cat pattern**

**1** Bend the bear into a sitting position with its right arm upraised. Blush the cheeks. Tie the fabric strip around the neck in a shoestring bow (see page 141) with 1¼" loops and 2½" tails. Cut the twine in half and thread each half through the holes of a button. Knot and trim the ends to ½". Glue the buttons to the bear's tummy.

**2** Paint the dowel white to represent chalk. Use the paint marker to write "My teacher is "Beary" Special" on the slate. Draw a cat in the top right corner; work a sum and write alphabet letters along the bottom. Glue the apple to the left top. Glue the chalkboard between the bear's right arm and leg. Glue the chalk into the right paw and the eraser into the left paw.

# Teacher Slate

### by Marilyn Gossett

one 7½"x5½" slate with wooden frame
drill, ¹⁄₁₆" bit
4 pencils bundled together with rubber bands
¾" tall wooden letters: T, E, A, C, H, E, R
1¾" tall wooden boy
2¾" tall wooden schoolhouse
white paint marker
black fine-tip permanent pen
acrylic paints: pale peach, golden yellow, red, blue, brown
#4 flat paintbrush
walnut acrylic stain, soft cloth
36" of 20-gauge black wire, needlenose pliers
low temperature glue gun and sticks or tacky craft glue

**1** Drill a hole in each top corner of the slate. Apply stain to the frame; wipe off excess. Insert one wire end through one hole in the frame, back to front. Use the pliers to twist the end into a small circle. Wrap the long end around the pencils to coil it. Remove the pencils. Bend and stretch the coils slightly, then insert the end through the other hole and secure as before. Use the paint marker to write the message on the slate.

**2** Paint the letters, schoolhouse and boy as shown. Mix equal parts brown paint and water to blush the boy's cheeks. Dip dot (see page 143) a green bell and a blue doorknob. Paint yellow squares for windows and a rectangle for the sign. Use the black pen to draw the boy's eyes and mouth, to draw the stitching lines on all the pieces and to write "School" on the sign. Glue the pieces to the frame as shown.

# Gold Leaf Pot

by LeNae Gerig

6¾" wide terra cotta pot
acrylic paints: royal blue, navy blue, gold
gold leaf, gold leaf adhesive
acrylic spray sealer
old toothbrush
small sea sponge
paper plate
paper towels
paintbrushes: 1" sponge, #10 flat brush
seven 1" wide wooden stars
5 cups of blue/purple/burgundy potpourri
    with gold-brushed pine cones

(**Note:** When working with gold leaf it is important not to breathe in any flaking metal; a filter mask is helpful.)

**1** Spray the pot with sealer to prevent too much paint absorption. Use the sponge brush to paint the pot royal blue inside and out; let dry. Moisten the sea sponge, pour navy paint onto a paper plate, dip the sponge into the paint and blot on a paper towel. Sponge the pot sides and let dry.

**2** Use a clean sponge brush to apply adhesive to the pot rim. Let dry until tacky. Tear off ½"–1" pieces of gold leaf. Use your fingers to apply them to the pot, then smooth out wrinkles with a clean dry flat brush.

**3** Moisten the toothbrush and dip it into gold paint. Use your thumb to pull the bristles back to spatter paint onto the pot sides as shown. Let dry. Spray the pot with sealer and let dry.

**4** Fill the pot with potpourri. Paint the stars gold and let dry. Sprinkle the stars over the potpourri.

# Candle in a Dish

by Marilyn Gossett

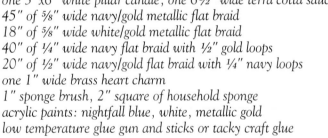

one 3"x6" white pillar candle, one 6½" wide terra cotta saucer
45" of ⅝" wide navy/gold metallic flat braid
18" of ⅝" wide white/gold metallic flat braid
40" of ¼" wide navy flat braid with ½" gold loops
20" of ½" wide navy/gold flat braid with ¼" navy loops
one 1" wide brass heart charm
1" sponge brush, 2" square of household sponge
acrylic paints: nightfall blue, white, metallic gold
low temperature glue gun and sticks or tacky craft glue

**1** Use the sponge brush to paint the saucer blue; let dry. Moisten the sponge, dip it in white paint, and lightly sponge over the blue. Repeat with gold paint.

**2** Glue ⅝" navy braid around the rim of the saucer, ⅝" white braid below the rim and gold loop braid around the bottom, loops up.

**3** Glue four vertical rows of ⅝" braid evenly spaced around the candle. Glue gold loop braid between the rows, with the loops facing away from the center front and center back.

**4** Glue navy loop braid around the candle top and bottom, loops up. Glue the charm as shown. Set the candle in the saucer as shown in the large photo.

# Dot Appliqué Shirts

**basic supplies:**
- dimensional paints
- black pen
- shirt board or plastic-covered cardboard
- waxed paper
- white paper
- straight pins
- ruler
- fabric glue

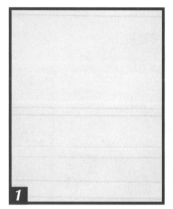

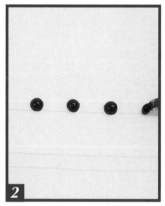

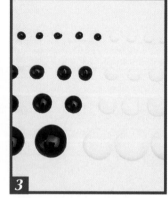

**1** Use the ruler and pen to draw two parallel lines ½" apart on the white paper. Repeat to make line pairs ⅜" apart, ¼", ³⁄₁₆", ⅛" and ¹⁄₁₆". These will be your guides for squeezing dots. Lay a sheet of waxed paper over the ruled lines.

**2** Shake the paint into the bottle tip (it helps to store the bottle upside down). Squeeze the bottle, applying gentle pressure until the dot grows to the needed size.

**3** Referring to the project supplies, squeeze the required colors and sizes of dots onto the waxed paper. Let them dry overnight.

**4** Insert the shirt board into the shirt to protect it from excess glue. Use a straight pin to pick up each dot from the waxed paper. Squeeze a dot of fabric glue onto the shirt, then place the point dot in the glue. (Dots will stick to one another, so glue is not needed when applying dots over other dots.)

# Footprints Shirt

### by Mary Carroll

*basic supplies (see above)*
*white t-shirt*
*shiny black dimensional paint dots:*
- *thirty-five ½"*
- *thirty-five ¼"*
- *seventy ³⁄₁₆"*
- *thirty-five ⅛"*

Position the dots first, then glue in place after you are satisfied with the arrangement. Refer to the large photo to position the ½" dots on the shirt in a staggered row—place one on the right sleeve. Add a ¼" dot to each foot for a big toe, two ³⁄₁₆" dots for the middle toes, and a ⅛" dot for the little toe.

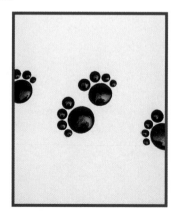

# Little Lambs Shirt

by Mary Carroll

*basic supplies (see page 54)*
*green t-shirt*
*shiny white dimensional*
*   paint dots:*
*   • fourteen ½"*
*   • fourteen ⅜"*
*   • twenty-eight ¼"*
*   • forty-eight ⅛"*
*   • two ¹⁄₁₆"*
*   • one hundred ninety-six ¼"–⅜" (wool)*
*shiny black dimensional paint dots:*
*   • one ½"*
*   • one ⅜"*
*   • two ¹⁄₁₆"*
*   • twenty-eight ¼"–⅜" (wool)*

**1** Refer to the large photo for the placement of the sheep. The top row of seven faces left, the bottom row right. Both the rows and the sheep in each row are 1¼" apart. **For each white sheep:** Place a ½" dot for each body and a ⅜" dot for each head, overlapping the head slightly on the body. Place 6–8 "wool" dots on each head and each body, overlapping them for a woolly texture.

**2** Place two ¼" dots for legs and a ⅛" dot for the tail. Place two ¹⁄₁₆" black dots for eyes. Place ⅛" white dots evenly spaced between the sheep and at the end of each row. Place a row of eight evenly spaced ⅛" dots 1" above the top row and another 1" below the bottom row.

**3** **For the black sheep:** Use black dots for the body, legs, tail and wool. Use white dots for the eyes.

# Placemat & Napkin Sets by Marilyn Gossett

**for each placemat, napkin and napkin ring set:**
*low temperature glue gun and sticks*
*fabric glue*
*sewing machine (optional)*
*one 16¾" square black napkin*

**for the ivory set:**
*one 14½"x20" ivory fringed woven placemat*
*one 2"x1" black wooden napkin ring*
*brass heart charms: three 1", two ⅝" wide*
*1½ yard of ⅝" wide black/gold braid*
*¾ yard of ½" wide ivory/gold braid*
*⅞ yard of ¾" wide black/gold braid*
*2 yards of ¾" wide white/gold edging*

**for the black set:**
*one 12¾"x17¾" black cotton placemat with a 15"x10" pleated inset*
*one 2"x1½" brass napkin ring*
*3¾ yards of ⅝" wide black/gold edging*
*1⅔ yards of ¾" metallic gold and black braid*

**1 Ivory set:** Glue ⅝" black braid along each short edge of the mat, just inside the fringe. Glue ½" ivory braid inside the first lengths and ¾" black braid inside the ivory lengths. Glue ⅝" black braid on each long edge, just inside the fringe, turning the ends under and covering the ends of the short lengths. Glue a 1" charm to the top left and bottom right corner; glue a ⅝" charm into each remaining corner.

**2** Napkin: Glue ¾" ivory edging around the outside edges, folding out the fullness at the corners and turning the ends under. Napkin ring: Glue ¾" black braid around the center. Glue a 1" charm to cover the seam. Fold the napkin and insert into the ring.

**3 Black set:** Glue ⅝" black edging around the mat so it extends ½" beyond the edge. Fold out the fullness in the corners and turn the ends under. Glue ¾" black braid around the pleated inset.

**4** Napkin: Glue ⅝" black edging round the outside as for the placemat. Finish the corners as for the placemat. Napkin ring: Glue ¾" black braid around the center. Fold the napkin and insert into the ring.

# Gold Sponged Set

by Marilyn Gossett

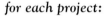

box top rosette

**for each project:**
1" sponge brush
2" square of household sponge
acrylic paints: black, metallic gold
matte acrylic sealer
low temperature glue gun and sticks or tacky
    craft glue

**for the potpourri pot:**
one 4¼" wide terra cotta pot
15" of ⅝" wide black/gold braid
15" of ⅝" wide black/gold loop edging
9" of ⅜" wide black/gold braid
one 2" wide white crocheted heart doily
one ¾" wide black ruffled ribbon rose
one 1" wide white ribbon rose
buttons: two ¾" black/gold hearts, one ½"
    gold heart in a heart
white acrylic paint
fine sandpaper
2 cups of decorative potpourri

**for the bottle:**
one 4½" tall octagonal spice bottle
12" of ¾" wide white/gold braid
12" of ¼" wide black/gold braid
three ½" gold rose buttons

**for the box:**
one 3¼"x5"x1½" papier-mâché book box
11" of ⅝" wide white/gold braid
22" of ¼" wide black/gold braid
11" of ¼" wide black/gold rose trim
12" of ⅝" wide black/gold loopy braid
ivory acrylic paint
one ⅝" brass heart button or charm

**1** Lightly sand the pot. Separate the bottle and cork. Seal each piece; let dry. Paint each piece black, including the inside of the box. Let dry. Moisten the sponge, dip in white paint and lightly sponge over the black. Repeat with metallic gold. Let dry; seal again.

**2** **Pot:** Glue loop edging around the lower rim, loops extending down. Glue ⅝" braid around the rim and ⅜" braid around the pot bottom. Glue the doily, roses and buttons to the pot front as shown in the photo. Fill with potpourri.

**3** **Bottle:** Glue one end of the ¾" braid to the inside rim of the bottle. Wrap the braid down the bottle front, under the bottom and up the other side. Glue the other end inside the rim opposite the first. Wrap the ¼" braid around the bottle neck and tie in a shoe-string bow (see page 141) with ¾" loops and 1½" tails. Glue the buttons in a triangle to the cork top; place it in the bottle.

**4** **Box:** Glue ¼" braid around the box bottom and the inner edge of the lid, turning the ends under. Glue the ⅝" white braid around the center of the box sides. Glue the rose trim above the white braid. Glue the heart to the center front. Coil the loopy braid into a 1½" wide medallion (see inset photo) and glue to the center top lid.

# Countdown Chalkboard

**by Tracia & Katelyn Ledford**

one 7½"x9½" chalkboard with wood-
  en frame
one 3¾" wide wooden star
five 1¼" wide wooden stars
spring-type wooden clothespin
acrylic paints: white, golden yellow,
  orange, black, brown, green
paintbrushes: #8 flat, #1 liner
1"x26" strip of red/green/ivory
  checked fabric
black fine-tip permanent pen
low temperature glue
  gun and sticks or
  tacky craft
  glue

**1** Paint the chalkboard frame
brown. Paint each of the stars
yellow and the clothespin green.
Let dry.

**2** Thin white paint with an
equal amount of water. Use the
liner brush to paint the numbers on
the board (you can draw them first
with chalk for guidelines.) Dip dot
(see page 143) the ends of the
strokes with undiluted white as
shown.

**3** Transfer (see page 143) the
snowman pattern to the large
star. Paint his body white, his arms
brown, and his nose and heart
orange. Dip dot black eyes, mouth
and buttons. Use the pen to draw
stitch lines around each star. Glue
the stars and clothespin to the
chalkboard as shown.

**4** Cut off 14" of the fabric strip
and glue the ends to the back
of the chalkboard to make a hanger. Use the rest to tie a shoestring
bow (see page 141) with 2" loops
and 2" tails. Glue to the center top.

# Perky Pens or Push Pins by Chere Brodsky

**for each:**
pencil and 1" of ⅛" wide elastic OR push pin
low temperature glue gun and sticks or tacky craft glue

**for the bunny:**
pom poms: one 1" white, two ¼" white, one ¼" pink
2½" square of white felt
two 3mm black beads
2" of monofilament nylon fishing line
pink powdered blush, cotton swab

**bunny ear**

**for the bird:**
blue pom poms: one ¾", one 1"
1"x⅜" piece of gold felt
two 3mm wiggle eyes
one 3" long blue feather

**bird beak**

**for the mouse:**
gray pom poms: one ¾" one ¾"
felt: 1" square of pink, 2" square of gray
8" of burgundy embroidery floss
three 3mm black beads
pink powdered blush, cotton swab

**mouse ears**

**penguin beak**

**for the penguin:**
pom poms: one 1" black, one ½" white
felt: ¾" square of gold, 2½" square of white
two 4mm black half-round beads

**1** **For each:** First make the head, then glue it onto a push pin or attach to a pencil with elastic: Glue the ends of the elastic together, forming a loop, then glue the loop into the back of the pom pom head. **Bunny:** Glue the ¼" white pom poms side by side to the front of the 1" for a muzzle. Glue the pink pom pom for a nose. Glue the beads for eyes. Cut two ears from felt, fold in half lengthwise and glue into the head. Blush the inner ears. Cut the fishing line into ¼" lengths and glue for whiskers.

**2** **Bird:** Glue the small pom pom into the center front of the large one. Fold the felt in half crosswise and cut a beak. Glue the fold into the center of the small pom pom. Glue the eyes above the beak. Cut the feather into three 1" lengths and glue for a tail.

**3** **Mouse:** Glue the ¼" pom pom into the ¾" as shown. Glue beads for eyes and a nose. Blush the cheeks. Loop the floss around your fingers, forming two 1½" loops. Remove, pinch the center to form a bow shape and glue the center under the nose. Cut a large heart from gray felt and two small hearts from pink felt. Glue as shown. Glue the point of the gray heart to the back of the head.

**4** **Penguin:** Glue the white pom pom into the center of the black. Cut the beak from felt and glue the straight edges together. Glue the beak into the head; glue the eyes above the beak.

# Ivory & Gold Tray by Marilyn Gossett

one 8¾"x15" wooden tray
50" of ½" wide
    green/metallic gold flat
    braid
acrylic paints: ivory, metal-
    lic gold
satin acrylic sealer
1" sponge brush, 2" square
    of household sponge
low temperature glue gun
    and sticks or tacky craft
    glue

**1** Use the sponge brush to paint the tray ivory. Moisten the sponge square and lightly dab gold paint over the ivory. Let dry; seal.

**2** Glue the trim around the center of the tray sides ½" below the top edge.

# Photo Album with Frame by Marilyn Gossett

one 7"x5" ivory photo album
one 7"x5" white photo mat
12" of ⅜" wide green satin picot ribbon
½ yard of ⅛" wide green cord
24" of ½" wide burgundy/metallic gold flat braid
burgundy ribbon roses: one 1½" wide, one 1" wide
    ruffled
buttons: four ½" wide metallic gold, one ¾" wide
    black/white cameo, one ½" brass leaf
1" sponge brush, 2" square of household sponge
low temperature glue gun and sticks or tacky craft
    glue

**1** Paint the mat ivory; let dry. Moisten the sponge and dab metallic gold lightly and evenly over the album and mat; let dry. Glue the mat to the album front, aligning the edges—leave an opening at the top to insert a photo.

**2** Glue the cord around the inner edges of the mat. Glue braid around the outer edges, cutting the corners diagonally to fit.

**3** Glue the small rose and two gold buttons to the lower right corner. Glue the large rose and the remaining buttons to the top left corner. Use the green ribbon to make a shoestring bow (see page 141) with 1" loops and 1½" tails. Trim the tails diagonally and glue the bow to the top left corner as shown.

# Doily Wall Hanging

by LeNae Gerig

three 4" round ivory crocheted doilies
18" of ⅝" wide ivory satin ribbon
2 yards of ¼" wide ivory satin ribbon
2 yards of ⅛" wide burgundy satin ribbon
three 1½" wide burgundy paper roses, each with a 1" long
    leaf
3" long ivory bell tassel
¼ oz. ivory larkspur
¼ oz. white dried baby's breath
¼ oz. light green dried plumosus
gold charms: 1¼" long cherub, 1¾" long key, ⅞" long
    heart
low temperature glue gun and sticks or tacky craft glue

**1** Fold one end of the ⅝" wide ribbon back and glue to form a 2" long loop. Glue a doily at the base of the loop and two more spaced ¼" apart down the ribbon as shown.

**2** Glue the tassel to the end of the ribbon under the last doily. Cut the ¼" ivory and burgundy ribbons each into three 24" lengths. Hold one length of each color together and make a loopy bow (see page 140) with four 2" loops and 3" tails. Repeat for two more bows. Glue a bow to the center of each doily.

**3** Cut each rose/leaf stem to ½" long. Glue one to each bow center, alternating the leaf directions as shown in the large photo. Cut the larkspur into 1"–1½" sprigs and glue around the roses.

**4** Cut the plumosus into 1"–3" sprigs and the baby's breath into 1"–2" sprigs. Glue among the bow loops and larkspur. Glue the cherub below the top rose, the key to the upper right of the middle rose and the heart to the lower left of the bottom rose as shown in the large photo.

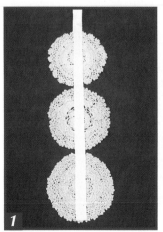

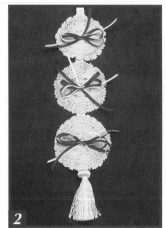

# Fancy Headbands by Marilyn Gossett

**for each headband:**
*one ¼" wide plastic headband*
*low temperature glue gun and sticks or tacky craft glue*

**for the rose headband:**
*six ¾" wide beige ribbon roses*
*24" of ¾" wide beige beaded flat lace*
*2 yards of ⅜" wide beige satin picot ribbon*

**for the ivory/gold headband:**
*2 yards of ⅜" ivory satin ribbon*
*16" of 6" wide ivory tulle net with flocked dots*
*12" of ⅛" wide metallic gold cord*
*16" of ⅞" wide ivory taffeta ribbon with metallic gold dots and edges*
*three ¾" wide metallic gold ribbon roses*
*white cloth-covered wire*

**1** **Rose headband:** Cut two 3" ribbon lengths. Wrap and glue one around each end of the headband. Tightly wrap the remaining ribbon spiral fashion around the headband, overlapping the wraps and gluing to secure. Trim off the excess ribbon.

**2** Glue one end of the lace to one end of the headband. Loop the lace along the top of the headband, gluing every ¾". Glue the roses between the loops along the center of the headband.

**3** **Ivory/gold headband:** Follow step 1 to cover the headband with ivory ribbon. Gather the tulle lengthwise and wire in the middle to form a "bow." Use the gold cord to make a loopy bow (see page 140) with four 1½" loops and ½" tails. Glue crosswise to the center of the tulle bow.

**4** Use the dotted ribbon to make a loopy bow with two 2" loops, two 1¾" loops and 1" tails. Glue to the center of the tulle bow. Glue the roses to the dotted bow center. Glue the bow to one side of the headband as shown in the photo.

# Eucalyptus Candle Ring by Karin Hupp

one 8" green preserved eucalyptus wreath
2 stems of burgundy silk rosebuds, each with five 1" long
  buds
8 sets of burgundy-edged green silk rose leaves, each with
  three 2" long leaves
1 stem of white fabric gypsophila with 12 sprigs, each with
  two 1½" long sections of ⅛" wide blossoms
3"x9" white pillar candle
low temperature glue gun and sticks or tacky craft glue

**1** Fluff the eucalyptus wreath, pulling sprigs of leaves up and outward to conceal the wire frame.

**2** Cut the gypsophila into twelve 2"–3" sprigs. Glue evenly spaced around the wreath, alternating them to angle to the inside and outside of the wreath.

**3** Cut the rosebuds with 1" stems and glue evenly spaced among the gypsophila sprigs, alternating them at opposing angles.

**4** Glue the leaves to fill any empty spaces among the gypsophila and rosebuds, angling some forward and some outward. Insert the candle as shown in the photo.

# Dip Dot Candle & Saucer by Teri Stillwaugh

4" wide terra cotta saucer, 3"x6" ivory pillar candle
acrylic paints: pale yellow, yellow ochre, white, mauve, light green
1" sponge paintbrush
⅛" wide paintbrush handle or stylus (for dip dots—see page 143)
paper plate, paper towels, fine sandpaper, acrylic spray sealer
soft cloth, rubbing alcohol

**1** **To prepare the candle:** Use the cloth to remove scratches and gloss from the candle surface, then moisten it with alcohol and wipe the entire candle; let dry. Mist with sealer; let dry. **To prepare the saucer:** Sand lightly, then seal all surfaces. Paint pale yellow inside and out; let dry.

**2** Refer to the photo to paint hearts and flowers evenly spaced over the surfaces of the candle and saucer. **For each heart:** Place two white dip dots so they just touch. Drag the second dot down at an angle, lifting the brush handle as you drag, to form the point. Place another dot below the heart point.

**3** **For each flower:** Pour out a ½" puddle each of yellow ochre, mauve and green paint. Place a yellow ochre dot for the center. Wipe the brush handle and make six evenly spaced mauve dots around the center for petals. Dot and drag as for the hearts to make three green leaves on each side. Let dry, then set the candle i the saucer.

The Kellys

The Anderson Family

# Tree Treasures

The Christmas tree provides warmth in a home, adding a festive feeling to the entire season. Bedecked in beautiful ornaments, touched with gold and silver, it becomes the focal point within the home and a gathering place for family members throughout the holidays. From the sweet to the sublime, we've included fun and creative ornaments to add cheer to any Christmas tree.

The Tangled Teddy, page 70, the Tin Soldier, page 69, and the Christmas Sock on page 71 are whimsical additions to a tree or a wreath, all cleverly created from polymer clay. A couple of snowmen also add a charming touch to the tree. The Frosty Fellow on page 95 is easy to create from a flat sheet of clay, while the Snowman on page 96 is simple shapes, joined to create a more rounded, playful companion.

Fabric yo-yos, purchased or made with your choice of fabrics, are used in the Christmas Ball on page 83 and the Calico Tree, page 84. Cream fabrics and ribbons, along with pearls, provide an elegant and romantic flavor to the ball. Bright, bold Christmas prints used for the calico tree allow it to contrast with the green branches of a Christmas tree, adding color and cheer.

These ornaments aren't just for the tree. They can decorate a wreath or garland, be tucked among the loops of a bow or tied onto a package for that special someone. They are made to delight—whether they deck the tree or other festive places!

shown actual size

# Tea Time by Jean Wiggins

*polymer clay: pink, yellow*
*1 ¼" wide brass heart stencil with scallops and flowers (American Traditional #FS-824)*
*½ paper clip, 5" of metallic gold thread (hanger)*
*round wooden toothpick, waxed paper, baking sheet, oven*
*optional: gloss lacquer*

**teapot**

1 Place waxed paper over the teapot pattern. Roll a 1" ball of pink clay and flatten to match the pattern, making the center about ⅜" thick and the edges thinner but rounded.

2 Press the stencil heart onto the teapot, lift the waxed paper and press gently from the back of the heart, forcing the clay through the stencil for a puffy appearance. Push harder in the center to round the pot—be careful not to push too much clay through, or the scallops will pull off when you remove the stencil. Press the stencil down around the flower designs, one at a time. Apply pressure all the way around the pot, a section at a time. Lift the stencil off carefully. Use your fingertip to rub out any unwanted areas of the design.

**base (top view)**  **lid (top view)**

3 Flatten a ⅜" ball of pink clay to match the base pattern and a ⅜" yellow ball to match the lid pattern. Press in place. Roll a 3/16" pink ball and press into the lid center for a knob.

**handle**  **spout**

4 **Handle:** Roll a ⅛"x2" yellow rope, slightly thinner on one end. Press the wide end onto the top right of the pot just below the lid. Curve it down and attach the narrow end near the bottom, curling it as shown. Flatten a ½" yellow ball to match the spout pattern, press onto the left side and use a toothpick to imprint a pouring hole. Insert the paper clip hanger into the top behind the lid knob. Remove from the waxed paper to a baking sheet and bake at 265° for one hour; let cool. Insert the gold thread through the paper clip and knot the ends together. Optional: Lacquer for a shiny ceramic look.

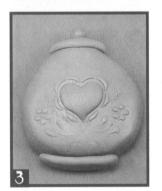

Wiggins
Judith Barker ©1987 FS-824

# Hanging Hearts by Jean Wiggins

*polymer clay: red, fluorescent red*
*1 ⅛" wide brass heart stencil with scallops (American Traditional #FS-824)*
*¾ yard of ⅛" wide white satin ribbon*
*⅜ yard of ⅛" wide red satin ribbon*
*6" of 3mm white fused pearls*
*two 1" long eye pins, waxed paper, round wooden toothpick, baking sheet, oven*

1 Blend a 1" ball of each red; divide in half. **For each heart:** Place waxed paper over the pattern. Roll half the clay into a cone, flatten and shape to match the pattern—keep the center ½" thick, the edges slightly thinner. Follow step 2 above to imprint the heart. Insert an eye pin into the center top.

2 Place the hearts on a baking sheet and bake at 265° for one hour; let cool. Cut a 12" and a 14" length of white ribbon. Insert one through the eye pin of each heart, then knot 2½" from the ends. Lay the knots together with the tails in opposite directions; lay the pearls over them, slightly off center. Tie the red ribbon around them in a shoestring bow (see page 141) with 1½" loops and 3" tails.

each heart 1¾" wide

# Mosaic Ornaments

## by Gail Ritchey

white polymer clay
ceramic tile, oven
X-acto® knife
stylus or round wooden toothpick
pasta machine set to #4, or rolling
pin and 2 craft sticks

**for the wreath:**
polymer clay: red, green
3" wide wreath stencil (American
Traditional #BL-22)
12" of 1/16" wide red satin ribbon
gloss lacquer

**for the tree:**
polymer clay: burgundy, forest
green
3" wide tree/holly stencil
(American Traditional #BL-04)
12" of 1/16" wide burgundy satin
ribbon

**1** **Wreath:** Roll a 1/2" red clay ball to 1/16" thick. Place the bow area of the wreath stencil over the red clay and use the stylus to press down around the edges, creating an imprint on the clay.

**2** Set the stencil aside. Use the knife to cut out the pieces. Lift them one at a time, smooth the cut edges and place the pieces on the tile. Roll a 1"

green ball to 1/16" thick, and make the holly leaves as for the bow. Bake the leaves and bow at 265° for 30 minutes; let cool. Remove from the tile.

**3** Roll a 1" white ball to 1/16" thick—at least a 3½" circle— and place on the tile. Place the stencil on the circle and use the stylus to trace inside the edge of each opening. Place the baked bow and holly pieces on the white layer, matching the imprints.

**4** Use the knife to trim the white clay within 1/4" of the wreath; also trim out the center hole. Use the stylus to poke two holes 1/4" apart at the center top. Bake the wreath for 30 minutes more; let cool. Insert the ribbon through the holes and knot the ends together for a hanger.

**Tree:** Make the tree ornament as for the wreath ornament, referring to the large photo for colors and placement.

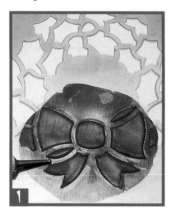

actual height 2⅜"

# Sparkle the Snowman

## by Jean Wiggins

 **nose**

*polymer clay: white, black,*
*    orange, yellow, brown,*
*    red, green*
*2 black seed beads (eyes)*
*1" long gold eye pin*
*darning needle*
*⅜" wide jingle bell*
*paper clip*
*gloss lacquer*
*fine iridescent glitter*  ○
*waxed paper*  ○
*baking sheet, oven*

**arm or**        **body**
**leg**

**head**

side view

**1 Legs:** Shape two ¾" white clay balls into 1½" teardrops. Place on waxed paper, points together and blunt ends extending outward at right angles. **Body:** Shape a 1¼" white ball into a pear. Attach over the points of the legs, pushing the center forward so the tummy falls between the thighs. **Arms:** Shape two ⅝" white clay balls into 1" teardrops. Attach the points behind the shoulders. Curve the arms down and forward to almost touch the legs.

**2 Head:** Roll a ⅝" white ball and flatten slightly. Attach to the neck. **Hat:** Flatten a ½" black ball to 1" across, press onto the top of the head and curve the sides slightly upward. Roll a ½"x½" black cylinder and attach to the top, shaping a slightly tapered crown. **Carrot nose:** Pinch a 3/16" orange ball into a ¼" long cone and attach to the face.

**3** Insert the beads for eyes; use the paper clip to imprint a curved mouth. **Holly:** Place waxed paper over the leaf pattern and flatten a ⅜" green ball to match; repeat. Use the needle to draw vein lines. Attach to his left shoulder as shown. Roll three ⅛" red balls and attach for berries. **Mistletoe:** Roll four 1/16"–⅛" green balls and flatten into ovals. Attach to the right hat brim extending in random directions. Roll three 1/16" white balls and attach over the leaves.

 **mistletoe**

**4 Buttons:** Roll two ⅛" black balls, flatten and press onto his tummy. **Broom:** Shape a 3/16"x1" brown log and round one end. Flatten a ⅜" yellow ball to match the bristle pattern and attach to the flat end. Use the needle to draw the lines. Roll a 1/16"x⅝" brown rope and wrap across the top of the bristles as shown on the pattern. Attach the broom as shown, keeping the handle straight. Insert the eye pin into the top of the hat. Use the bottom of the bell to imprint random snowflakes over the legs, arms and body. Bake at 265° for one hour; let cool. Lacquer. While the lacquer is still tacky apply glitter to the imprints.

**broom**

**holly**

**hat crown**

**hat brim**

# Tin Soldier

## by Jean Wiggins

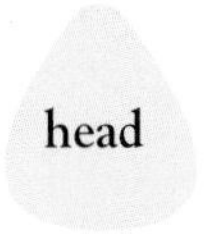

head

chest

pants

*polymer clay: navy blue, red, flesh, black, metallic gold*
*2 black seed beads*
*one 1" long gold eye pin*
*1½" of 20-gauge wire*
*X-acto® knife or sharp paring knife*
*darning needle*
*paper clip*
*waxed paper, baking sheet, oven*

actual height 4¼"

**1** Roll a ½"x2" navy log for the pants and a ½"x½" black log for the boots. Press the boots onto the pants bottom. Lay on waxed paper and flatten slightly. Use the needle to indent between the legs and feet as shown. Roll two ¹/₁₆"x2" red ropes and press one onto each side of the pants for stripes.

**2** Flatten a ¾" red ball to match the chest pattern; press onto the pants top. Flatten gold to ¹/₁₆" thick. Cut a ⅛"x1½", a ⅛"x½" and two ⅛"x2" strips. Place the ½" strip at his right waist extending up over his shirt—don't press it down. Wrap the 1½" strip around his waist for a sash; use the needle to imprint fold lines. Fold the ½" strip down over the sash. **Arms:** Roll two ¼"x1¼" red logs and flatten one onto each side of the body, rounding the upper ends into the shoulders. Roll two ¼" flesh balls, flatten slightly and attach for hands. Criss-cross the 2" gold strips over his chest as shown.

**3** Use the knife to cut fringe on the hanging end of the sash. **Epaulets:** Roll eight ¹/₁₆"x³/₁₆" gold ropes and lay four on each shoulder. Flatten a ¼" gold ball into a ⅛" thick oval. Cut it in half and press one half over the fringe on each side, curved side out. Roll four ¹/₁₆" gold balls for buttons. Flatten one onto the outside bottom of each sleeve and one on the outer top of each boot. Roll three ¹/₁₆" navy balls for shirt buttons; attach as shown. **Helmet:** Roll a ⅝"x¾" black log. Round the top; use your knuckle to press a hole into the bottom.

**4** **Head:** Roll a ⅝" flesh ball and shape the top to a point. Push the point into the helmet. Roll a ¹/₁₆" flesh ball and attach for his nose. Use the needle to pick up the seed beads and press above the nose for eyes. Use the end of the paper clip to imprint his mouth. Roll a ⅝"x1" black rope and wrap under his chin, attaching the ends to the helmet. Flatten a ¼" red ball to match the feather pattern and attach to the hat front. Use the needle to draw the shaft and vanes of the feather. Insert the wire length halfway into the bottom of his head, then insert the other end into the top of the body, firmly attaching the head to the shoulders. Insert the eye pin into the hat top. Bake at 265° for one hour; let cool.

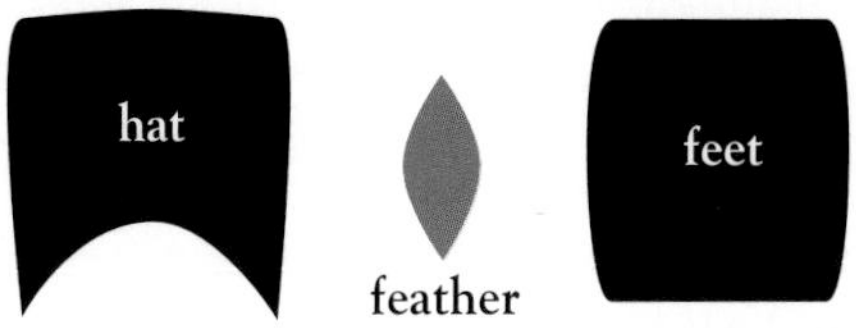

hat

feather

feet

actual
height
1½"

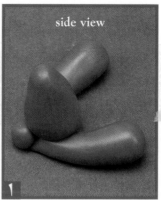

side view

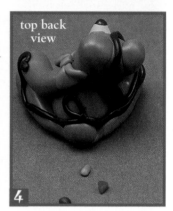

top back
view

# Tangled Teddy

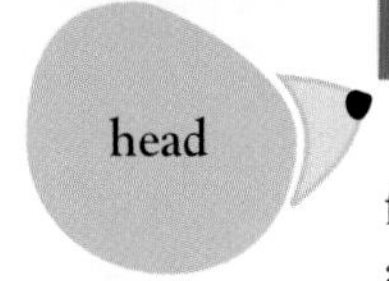

## by Jean Wiggins

*polymer clay: brown, white, black, green, red, blue, yellow*
*clay cutters: ⅛" heart, ½"x⅝" oval (or use the patterns*
*    below)*
*2 black seed beads*
*one 1" long eye pin*
*scrap of ⅛" dowel rounded on one end*
*waxed paper, darning needle, baking sheet, oven*

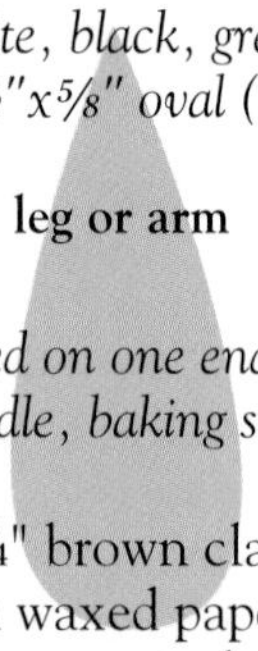

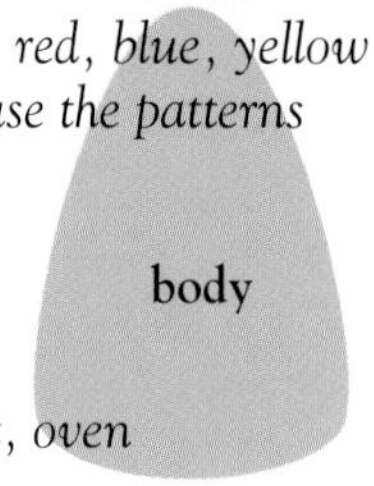

head

leg or arm

body

**1** **Legs:** Shape two ¾" brown clay balls into 1½"
teardrops. Place on waxed paper, points together
and blunt ends extending outward at right angles. **Tail:**
Roll a ⅜" brown ball and attach over the points of the
legs. **Body:** Shape a 1¼" brown ball into a pear. Attach
over the points of the legs, overlapping the tail as
shown, tipping it backward so the tummy protrudes.

**2** **Arms:** Shape two ⅝" brown clay balls into 1"
teardrops. Curve the neck to the left and attach
the points behind his shoulders. Use the side of the
needle to imprint paw marks in the end of each arm.
**Head:** Roll a ⅝" brown ball, pinch to a slight point at
the top and attach to the neck. Curve his right arm
down, then up, so the elbow rests on his knee and his
cheek rests on his paw. Curve his left arm down to
touch his leg. **Muzzle:** Blend a ¼" ball each of brown
and white to make tan. Roll two ³⁄₁₆" balls and set aside

for step 3. Shape the rest into a pointed muzzle and
attach to the face, tilting the point up. Use the needle
to draw the smile.

**3** Roll a ⅛" black ball and attach for his nose, pinching it to a point so it appears to grow out of his
muzzle. Insert the beads for eyes. Roll two ¼" balls for
ears. Cup each around the rounded end of the dowel and
attach firmly to the head, then pull the dowel out, leaving a depression in both the ear and the head. Use the
needle to poke a hole for his belly button. Flatten the
tan balls from step 2, press onto the soles of his feet and
use the needle to poke holes around them as shown.

**4** **Bow:** Flatten a ⅜" green ball into a ⅝" long oval;
cut in half. Curl the rounded end of each half
around the needle. Attach to the neck, curled ends
together. Flatten a ⅛" green ball into the bow center,
tuck the ends under and draw a knot line. **Lights:** Roll
a ¹⁄₁₆"x7" black rope. Wind it around the bear so he
looks all tangled up. Be sure it is in contact with his
body everywhere—loose sections may break. Shape a
socket with two very tiny (less than ¹⁄₁₆") prongs and
attach to one end of the cord. Flatten a ¹⁄₁₆" black ball
over the joined area for a plug. Roll about thirty ⅛"
balls of various bright colors, shape each into a teardrop
and attach at ¼" intervals. Insert the eye pin into the
top of his head. Bake at 265° for one hour; let cool.

plug ➤● light                    bow

# Christmas Sock

### by Jean Wiggins

*polymer clay: red, green, white, pink*
*2 black seed beads*
*12" of 2-gauge gold wire*
*10" of ⅛" wide red satin ribbon*
*10" of ⅛" wide white satin ribbon*
*pasta machine set to #1, or rolling pin*
*ruler, X-acto® knife or sharp knife, round pencil*
*darning needle, round wooden toothpick, tracing paper*
*waxed paper, baking sheet, oven*

**1 Sock:** Soften a 1½" ball of red clay and roll to ³⁄₁₆" thick. Cut five ⅜"x3½" strips. Repeat with green. Lay the strips side by side on waxed paper, alternating colors. Press together into a striped sheet as shown. Cut crosswise into ⅜" strips. Turn every other strip around to make a checkerboard pattern, press together and roll lightly.

**2** Trace the sock, heel and toe patterns; cut out. Place the sock pattern diagonally on the checkerboard and cut around it. Save the checked scraps for step 4. Use the scraps of flattened red left from step 1 to cut a heel and toe; press into place, smoothing the joints. Use the needle to imprint stitch marks around the heel and toe.

**3 Kitty:** Roll a ½" white ball into a cone. Lift the top of the sock and slip the cone under, pointed end down, to create the look of a body inside. Roll a ¼"x2½" log for the paws. Round the ends and thin the center. Attach to the top of the body. Roll a ¾" white ball for the head, shape to a slight point at the top and attach over the arms. Curve the paws over the sock top as shown; use the side of the needle to imprint toe lines in each paw. Roll two ¼" white balls and flatten side by side for a muzzle. Use the needle to prick whisker dots. Attach a ⅛" pink ball for a nose; insert the beads for eyes. Roll two ⅜" white balls and pinch into cones for ears. Press the side of the toothpick into the front of each ear to indent it; attach to the head.

**4 Bow:** Flatten two ¼" green balls to match the pattern. Attach point to point to the left shoulder. Insert the toothpick under each side of the bow to lift and curve it. Attach a ⅛" green ball for the knot. **Candy cane:** Roll a ³⁄₁₆"x2" rope each of red and white. Twist together and roll to smooth. Curve into a candy cane shape and trim the ends. Insert to the kitty's left. Flatten the checked scraps from step 2; attach over the back of the kitty and cane so the ornament back looks finished. Use the toothpick to poke a hole at each top corner of the sock. Bake at 265° for one hour; let cool. **Hanger:** Coil the wire around a pencil. Insert the ends through the holes and twist to secure. Hold the ribbon lengths together and knot around the hanger top, making a shoestring bow (see page 141) with 1½" loops and 2" tails.

actual height 4" excluding hanger

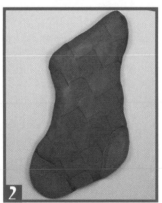

# Mini Birdhouse Ornaments by LeNae Gerig

**for each birdhouse:**
*fine sandpaper*
*drill with ¹⁄₁₆" bit*
*½" long eye pin*
*#6 flat paintbrush*
*tacky craft glue*
*9" of fine gold cord*

Lightly sand the rough edges of each house. Drill a hole ½" deep in the roof. Follow the directions below to decorate each birdhouse, then glue the eye pin into the hole, thread with gold cord and knot the ends to make a hanger.

**Noel House (left):**
*1¾"x2⅞" wooden birdhouse with a steep roof*
*acrylic paints: dark green, ivory, red*
*#1 liner paintbrush*
*round wooden toothpicks*

**1** Use the flat brush to paint the roof, hole and perch green. Paint the house sides ivory; let dry. Use the liner brush handle to make green dip dots (see page 143) around the base of the house and red dip dots along the front edge of the roof. Use a toothpick to make red dip dots around the hole.

**2** Use the liner with red paint to write "NOEL" in the center of each side of the roof. Use the liner handle to paint a heart in the upper left and lower right corner on each side. (To make dip-and-drag hearts, first make two dip dots side by side, then drag the second down diagonally, lifting the brush to make a point.)

**Spattered House (center):**
*2¼"x2¼" wooden birdhouse*
*acrylic paints: red, white, green*
*#1 liner paintbrush*
*old toothbrush*

**3** Use the flat brush to paint the house roof red, the sides white and the hole and perch green. Let dry, then lightly sand the roof edges. Use the liner brush to paint a green dip dot heart (see step 1) over the hole.

**4** Dip the toothbrush into water and then into green paint. Pull back the bristles to spatter paint over the house.

## Barn (page 72 right):
*2"x2" wooden barn birdhouse*
*½" wide wooden star*
*acrylic paints: ivory, dark red, light brown, brown, metallic gold*
*acrylic crackle medium*

**5** Use the flat brush to paint the barn roof, hole and perch light brown. Paint brown lines across the roof as shown. Follow the manufacturer's directions to apply crackle medium to the barn sides, let dry, then paint the sides red; the paint will crackle as it dries. Sand the roof edges to give the wood an aged look. Paint the star gold, let dry and glue to the peak of the roof.

## Ivory House with Gold Roof (left):
*2¾"x2¼" wooden birdhouse*
*acrylic paints: ivory, metallic gold*
*gold glitter spray*
*1" wide brass birds/heart charm*

Paint the roof, hole and perch gold with the house sides ivory. Let dry. Glue the charm over the hole and spray the house with glitter and let dry.

## Gingerbread House (center):
*2⅞"x2" wooden chalet birdhouse*
*acrylic paints: brown, white, red, green*
*textured snow paint*

**6** Paint the house roof, hole, perch and base white. Paint the sides brown and let dry. Use the brush handle to paint red and green dip dots around the hole. Rinse the brush and apply snow paint to the roof and base.

## Gold-Webbed House (right):
*2"x2½" wooden birdhouse*
*6" of ¼" wide metallic gold ribbon*
*½" wide brass heart charm*
*ivory acrylic paint*
*gold spray webbing*

Paint the house ivory and let dry. Spray the house with gold webbing and let dry. Use the ribbon to make a shoestring bow with ¾" loops and tails. Glue the bow to the center top of the house just below the eye pin. Glue the charm over the center of the bow.

actual height 4"

# Bear on a Ball

by Rosalie Evan

one ¾" wide red glass Christmas ball
tan pom poms: one 1½", seven 1", one ½"
three 6mm black half-round beads
9" of ⅛" wide white satin ribbon
one 4" long sprig of green vinyl pine
one ¾" wide white ribbon rose
needle, 9" of nylon monofilament fishing line
low temperature glue gun and sticks or tacky craft glue

**1** Glue the 1½" pom pom to the top of the glass ball to make a body and head.

**2** Glue four 1" pom poms for arms and legs. Glue the ½" pom pom to the bottom back of the ball for a tail.

**3** Glue the remaining 1" pom poms to the head as shown for ears and a muzzle.

**4** Glue the beads for the eyes and nose. Glue the pine sprig angling across the ball as if the bear were holding it. Use the ribbon to make a shoestring bow (see page 141) with ¾" loops and ¾" tails. Glue to the center of the pine sprig, then glue the rose to the bow center. **Hanger:** Thread the nylon line onto the needle, take a stitch through the top of the head and knot the ends together.

# Reindeer on a Bell

by Loyal Hjelmervik

pom poms: two 1" tan, four ½" tan,
  one ½" white
one 2" wide gold jingle bell
1 brown chenille stem
½"x1" piece of tan felt
three 3mm black half-round beads
¼ yard of ⅜" wide green satin
  ribbon
tracing paper, pencil, transfer paper
low temperature glue gun and sticks

ear

actual height 2¼"

**1** Glue one 1" pom pom on top of the other to make the head and body. Transfer the ear pattern twice onto the felt, reversing it the second time to make right and left ears. Pinch each ear at the base and glue into the head, placing the longer side toward the outside.

back view

**2** Cut four ⅞" chenille lengths. Twist two together to form a cross; repeat. Glue behind the ears for antlers. Glue the white pom pom for his muzzle. Glue beads for his eyes and nose.

**3** Turn the reindeer to face left. Glue the ½" tan pom poms as shown for his hands and feet.

**4** Glue the reindeer to the right side of the bell. Use the ribbon to make a shoe-string bow with ¾" loops, a 2" and a 3" tail. Glue it as shown, then ripple and glue the tails down the sides of the bell.

actual height 2"

# Joy Elves
### by Nancy Overmyer

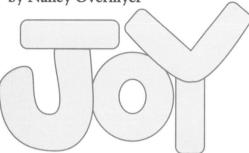

dough (see page 142): natural, light peach, green
9" of ⅛" wide red satin ribbon
acrylic paints: red, black, coral
#1 liner paintbrush
½ paper clip (hanger)
round wooden toothpick
waxed paper, aluminum foil
oven, baking sheet
polymer sealer

ear

hat

head

foot

leg

1 Roll a ¼"x8" natural dough rope. Lay waxed paper over the JOY pattern. Cut and bend sections of the rope to fit. Moisten the pieces to join them. Transfer the letters from the waxed paper to foil.

2 **Heads:** Roll two ½" peach balls and attach to the letters as shown. Roll four ³⁄₁₆" peach teardrops and attach for ears; indent with the toothpick. **Hands:** Roll two ⅛" peach balls. Attach one to the left side of the J and one to the right side of the Y.

3 **Hats:** Roll two ½" green balls into cones and attach one to each head. **Legs:** Roll three ¼"x1" green ropes and attach as shown. Roll three ⅛" natural balls, flatten and attach for shoes. Insert the hanger in the top of the J. Bake at 200° until hard (about three hours).

4 Paint the shoes red. Paint red candy cane stripes on the JOY. Use the toothpick to dip dot (see page 143) black eyes. Use the liner brush to paint the nose and mouth coral; let dry. Seal; let dry. Cut the ribbon in half and use each half to make a shoestring bow with ¼" loops and ⅜" tails. Glue one to each elf's neck.

# Tall Hat Santa

pom pom

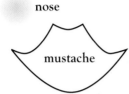
nose

mustache

by Nancy Overmyer

actual height 4"

1

2

3

dough (see page 142): natural, light peach, pink, red
9" of ⅛" wide red satin ribbon
acrylic paints: black, white
#1 liner paintbrush
pink powdered blush, cotton swab
one 1" long sprig of vinyl pine with holly
sharp knife
½ paper clip (hanger)
round wooden toothpick
aluminum foil
oven, baking sheet
polymer sealer
low temperature glue gun and sticks or tacky craft glue

face

hat

**1** **Head:** Roll a 1" ball of peach dough for the face. Roll a 1" ball of natural into a 2" long rope with tapered ends. Moisten with water and attach for the beard.

**2** Shape a ½" ball of natural to match the mustache pattern and attach to face. Attach a ¼" pink ball over the mustache for a nose. Use the knife to score hair lines on the beard and mustache.

beard

**3** **Hat:** Flatten a ½" ball of natural and attach to the top of the head for the brim. Roll a 1" red ball into a 2½" long cone and attach to the brim, curving the tip down as shown. Insert the hanger at the top of the curve. Attach a ½" ball of natural to the hat tip. Place on foil and bake at 200° for 4–5 hours. Let cool; blush the cheeks. Use the toothpick to dip dot (see page 143) black eyes and the liner brush to paint white eyebrows. Seal; let dry. Glue the pine sprig to the hat as shown in the large photo. Knot the ribbon through the hanger.

# Bag Full of Fun

### by Diane Bliss

craft foam: tan, red, white, blue
3" of 20-gauge gold wire
darning needle
18" of ¼" red/green/gold satin ribbon
X-acto® knife
¼" hole punch
tracing paper
pencil
transfer paper
black fine-tip permanent pen
E-6000™, Goop® or Delta® jewel glue

**1** Transfer (see page 143) the patterns and cut the pieces from the colors shown. Punch three blue dots. Use the pen to draw the outlines and detail lines. Personalize the bag with your name or the name of the intended recipients. Glue the muzzle on the bear. Glue the bag to the base, matching the bag top to the dashed line. Glue the stripes on the candy cane and the blue dots on the ball.

**2** **Bag neck:** Cut a slit along each of the heavy curving lines. Weave the ribbon through the slits, bringing one end to the front through each of the two right slits. Tie the ends in a shoestring bow with 1" loops and 2"–3" tails. Poke the wire through the bear's ear and twist the ends together to form a hanger.

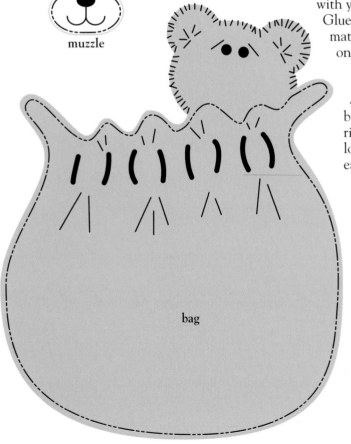

muzzle

bag

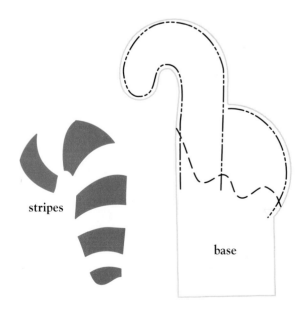

stripes

base

# Smokey the Cat

### by Diane Bliss

*craft foam: gray, red, white*
*12" long black chenille stem*
*black dimensional paint*
*⅝" white button*
*⅛" hole punch*
*tracing paper, pencil, transfer paper*
*black fine-tip permanent pen*
*E-6000™, Goop® or Delta® jewel glue*

**1** Transfer (see page 143) the patterns and cut the pieces from the colors shown. Use the pen to go over the outlines and the checked design on the hat. Use the dimensional paint to squeeze the remaining lines and dots. Let dry.

**2** Glue the forepaws and head to the body. Glue the hat to the top of the head. Glue the hat trim over the seam between the head and hat, with the tassel extending to the right. Glue the button on the tassel. Punch a hole in the right side of the tail and in the top of the left hip. Insert the ends of the chenille stems through the holes and twist to secure, forming an arched hanger.

actual height 4" excluding hanger

head

hat

Smokey

hat trim

forelegs and paws

body

actual height 6"

# Frosty Family

## by Diane Bliss

*craft foam: green, red, white, blue, yellow, black*
*12" of 1/16" wide white satin ribbon*
*darning needle*
*hole punches: 1/8", 1/4"*
*tracing paper, pencil, transfer paper*
*black fine-tip permanent pen*
*E-6000™, Goop® or Delta® jewel glue*

1 Transfer (see page 143) the patterns and cut the pieces from the colors shown (you may want to vary the number of snowpeople to fit your family). Punch four 1/4" red cheek dots and ten assorted 1/4" red, white, blue and yellow dots. Use the pen to go over the lines and to personalize the snowkids.

2 Glue the adult snowpeople and the star to the tree. Glue the top hat and tie on the left snowperson. Glue the cap trim to the right snowperson, placing it just above the eyes; glue the large cap above the trim and the scarf to the neck. Glue two cheeks on each snowperson. Glue the snowkids in a row along the bottom of the ornament. Glue a cap above each snowkid. Glue the remaining dots to the tree for ornaments. Punch a 1/8" hole in the top of the star, insert the ribbon and knot the ends to make a hanger.

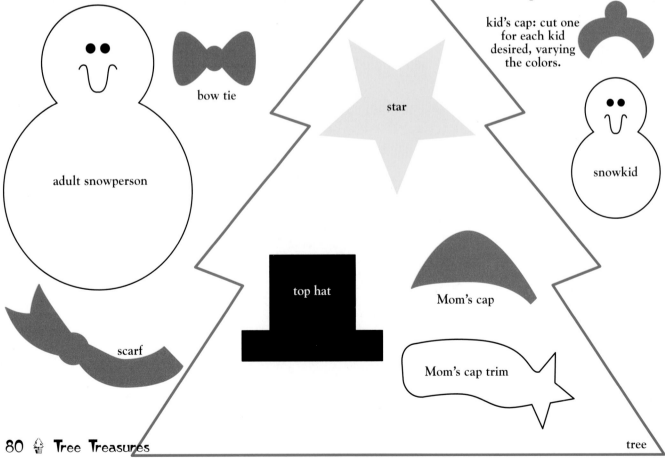

bow tie

adult snowperson

scarf

star

top hat

Mom's cap

Mom's cap trim

kid's cap: cut one for each kid desired, varying the colors.

snowkid

tree

# Snug in a Bed

### by Diane Bliss

craft foam: red, white, tan, assorted colors for caps
12" of ¹⁄₁₆" wide white satin ribbon
³⁄₈" wide pom poms: 1 for each cap, assorted colors
¹⁄₈" hole punch
tracing paper, pencil, transfer paper
black fine-tip permanent pen
E-6000™, Goop® or Delta® jewel glue

**bed**

**1** Transfer (see page 143) the patterns and cut the pieces from the colors shown (if you need more than three kids, you will need to widen the bed and blanket). Use the pen to go over the lines. Personalize the blanket and caps.

**2** Glue the blanket on the bed. Glue the heads, above the blanket, then the caps above the heads. Glue the pom poms on the caps, varying the colors. Punch a hole in the top of each bedpost. Insert one end of the ribbon through each hole, front to back, and knot the ends to secure them.

actual height 3½"

**blanket**

head:
cut 1 for
each kid

cap: cut 1 for each
kid, varying the colors

# Festive Mailbox Magnet

### by Diane Bliss

**mailbox front**

**mailbox post**

craft foam: red, black, blue, tan
12" of ¹⁄₈" wide green satin ribbon
black fine-tip permanent pen
white dimensional paint
tracing paper, pencil, transfer paper
E-6000™, Goop® or Delta® jewel glue

**1** Transfer (see page 143) the patterns and cut the pieces from the colors shown. Go over the lines with the pen; personalize the mailbox front.

**2** Glue the mailbox front to the back, then glue the mailbox to the post. Glue the bow below the mailbox. Glue the bow loops to the bow and the bow to the post. Use the dimensional paint to squeeze polka dots on the bow. Knot the ends of the ribbon together and glue the knot to the back for a hanger.

**bow**

mailbox
back: cut
1 of black

bow knot
and loops

actual
height
4½"

# Christmas Ball Ornament

by Joan Zeigler

*3" Styrofoam® ball*
*fifty 2" fabric circles in assorted white or off-white shades*
   *(or fifty 1" wide yo-yos)*
*1⅓ yards of ⅜" wide ivory satin ribbon*
*1 yard of ⅛" wide ivory satin ribbon*
*fifty 6mm white pearls*
*50 straight pins*
*one pearl-headed corsage pin*
*12" of thin gold cord*
*needle, ivory thread*
*low temperature glue gun and sticks of tacky craft glue*

**1** **For each yo-yo:** Sew a running stitch ⅛" from the outside edge of each fabric circle. Pull to gather tightly into a flat pouch with the right side of the fabric out. Knot the threads to secure. Make fifty yo-yos.

**2** Pin the circles through the centers to cover the ball, with the gathered sides out. Secure them with a drop of glue at each loose edge.

**3** Glue a pearl to the center of each yo yo.

**4** Knot the ends of the gold cord together; glue the knot to the center top of the ball. Cut 12" of the ⅜" ribbon and set aside. Hold the remaining ribbon together with the ⅛" ribbon and handle as one to make a loopy bow (see page 140) with four 3" loops and 6"–9" tails. Tie the center of the ribbon with the 12" length. Knot ½" from the end of each tail. Glue the bow to the top of the ball between the strands of the hanger. Insert the corsage pin through the bow center and the knot of the hanger.

# Calico Tree Ornament

### by Joan Zeigler

actual height

fabric circles in assorted red, white
    and green prints: two 2″, two 3″,
    two 4″, two 5″
one 1″ long cork
one ⅞″ wide brass star charm
4″ length of green chenille stem
8″ of thin gold cord
needle, ivory thread
low temperature glue gun or tacky
    craft glue

**1** Follow step 1 on page 82 to make each fabric circle into a yo-yo.

**2** Make a ¼″ deep hole in the wide end of the cork. Dip one end of the chenille stem in glue and insert into the hole.

**3** Snip a ⅛″ slit in the center of each yo-yo. With the gathered sides up, thread the yo-yos onto the stem, beginning with the largest and ending with the smallest. Vary the colors. Don't push the circles flat—let them puff.

**4** Cut the chenille stem ¾″ above the last yo-yo. Knot the ends of the gold cord and bend the stem over the cord. Glue the star to one side of the stem as shown in the large photo above.

actual height 4"

# Bear on a Goose

by Teresa Nelson

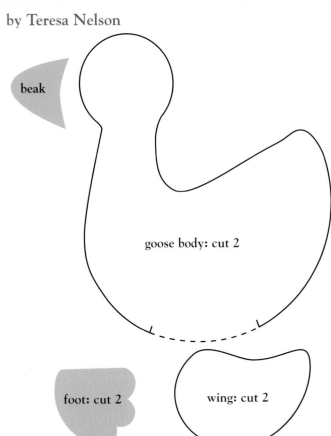

beak

goose body: cut 2

foot: cut 2

wing: cut 2

brown pom poms: two 1", four ½", three ¼"
five 4mm half-round beads
9" of ⅜" wide red grosgrain ribbon
felt: 2"x7" of white, 1"x3" of gold
needle, white thread
polyester fiberfill
tracing paper, pencil, transfer paper
9" of nylon monofilament fishing line
low temperature glue gun and sticks or tacky craft glue

**1** **Goose:** Transfer (see page 143) the patterns to the indicated felt colors and cut out. Pin the beak between the body pieces. Whipstitch (see page 144) the pieces together, leaving an opening at the body bottom. Stuff, then sew the opening closed. Glue on the feet.

**2** Glue a wing on each side of the goose. Glue a bead on each side of the head for eyes.

**3** **Bear:** Glue the 1" pom poms together for the head and body. Glue a ¼" pom pom for his muzzle and the other ¼" pom poms for his ears. Glue a bead for his nose and two beads for eyes. Glue him to the goose as shown.

**4** Glue the ½" pom poms for hands and feet as shown, with one hand on each side of the goose's neck. Use the ribbon to tie a shoestring bow (see page 141) with ½" loops and ¾" tails. Glue to the goose's neck. Thread the nylon line through the needle, take a stitch through the top of the bear's head and knot the ends together for a hanger.

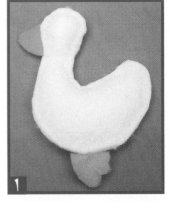

1

2

3

4

# Fancy Bunny

by Rosalie Evan

*pom poms: one 2" white, two ¾" white, one ¼" pink*
*two ¼" strips of doll eyelashes*
*two 6 mm black half-round beads*
*felt: 3" square of white, 2" square of pink*
*18" of 1" wide white ivory gathered lace*
*1½"x18" strip of blue calico fabric with pink flowers*
*12" of 1⅜" wide pink organza ribbon*
*9" of thin gold cord*
*needle, white thread*
*tracing paper, pencil*
*low temperature glue gun and sticks or tacky craft glue*

actual height 4"

**1** **Muzzle:** Glue two ¾" white pom poms side by side to the 2" pom pom; glue the ¼" pink pom pom over the seam for the nose.

**2** Trace and cut out the patterns. Cut two ears, two inner ears and two eyelids from the indicated felt colors. Glue each inner ear to an outer ear, pinch the bottom and glue to secure. Part the large pom pom and glue the ears into the top of the head.

**3** Glue the beads for eyes. Glue the eyelashes to the rounded edge of the eyelids, then glue over the eyes as shown.

**4** Lay the bound edge of the lace along one long edge of the fabric. Sew a running stitch ⅛" from the edge, pull to gather into a circle and knot to secure. Glue the head to the center of the circle. Use the ribbon to tie a shoestring bow (see page 141) with 1" loops and 3" tails. Glue at the right neck. Knot the ends of the gold cord together, part the pom pom between the ears and glue in the knot to make a hanger.

ear

inner ear

eyelid

# Cotton Glove Ornaments by Marilyn Gossett

snowman 4½" tall
reindeer 4" tall

**for each ornament:**
*one 2–3" long finger from a
  cotton work glove (1 pair of
  gloves will make 8–10 ornaments)*
*polyester fiberfill*
*pink powdered blush*
*cotton swab*
*#5 ivory perle cotton thread*
*needle*
*brush-on glitter glaze*
*#4 flat paintbrush*
*black fine-tip permanent pen*
*tracing paper, pencil*
*low temperature glue gun and
  sticks or tacky craft glue*

## Snowman:

*burgundy/black checked fabric: one 2¼"x4" piece, one ½" square*
*black/ivory checked fabric: one ½"x10" strip, one ½" square*
*cotton batting: one 5" circle, one 1"x5" strip*
*one ¾" wide wooden star, two 2" long twigs*
*three ¼" wide black snaps, one ⅜" wide green button*
*acrylic paints: black, orange, white, yellow*
*decorative snow paint*

**1 Body:** Sew a running stitch ⅛" in from the edge of the batting circle and pull to gather into a pouch. Stuff with fiberfill. Stuff the glove finger, glue the opening closed and insert into
the pouch opening with the top extending 1". Referring to the
pattern, use a toothpick to dip dot (see page 143) the eyes and
mouth. Blush the cheeks; dip dot white highlights on each.

**2** Paint the nose orange. Paint the wooden star yellow; outline
with the pen. **Hat:** Fold up and glue ¼" along one 4" edge of
the burgundy fabric. Wrap and glue around the head. Glue the seam
closed in back. Lightly stuff with fiberfill. Wrap with thread ¾" below
the hat top and knot to secure. Glue the star to the knot. Glue a
¼"x4" strip of cotton batting around the hat brim. **Scarf:** Tie the
½"x10" fabric strip around his neck; trim the tails diagonally.

**3 Mittens:** Trace the pattern and cut four from batting. Glue two
pieces together, sandwiching one end of a twig between them.
Repeat. Glue the twig arms into opposite sides of the snowman,
thumbs up. Glue the ½" fabric squares to the right front of the lower
body, overlapping them slightly. Glue a button to the patches. Glue
the snaps in a row down the front. Apply decorative snow in random
patches, then brush on glitter glaze.

tail

ear

5" circle

mitten

## Reindeer:

*two 2" squares of cotton batting*
*four 2¾" long cinnamon sticks*
*one 6" long sprig of green vinyl pine*
*two 2" sprigs of green preserved princess pine*
*one ¼" wide wooden plug*
*acrylic paints: brown, red, black*

**1 Body:** Cut a glove finger into a 2" and a
1" length. Stuff each length and sew the
openings closed. Match the stitched edges and
glue the two pieces together to form a 2" body
and 1" neck.

**2 Head:** Trace the patterns and cut two
heads, two ears and one tail from batting.
Whipstitch the head pieces together, leaving
the top open. Stuff; sew closed. Glue the top of
the head to the neck.

**3** Glue on the ears and tail. Paint the reindeer brown. Paint the wooden plug red
and glue for his nose. Use a toothpick to dip
dot black eyes. Wrap the vinyl pine stem
around his neck, twisting the ends to secure it.
Glue the princess pine for antlers.

**4 Legs:** Cut four ¼" slits in the bottom of
the reindeer. Glue a cinnamon stick into
each slit. Make sure the legs are balanced so he
can stand.

## Garden angel (top left):

one 2" wide straw hat
twelve 6" strands of blonde
    lil' Loopies™ doll hair
two ½" wide sprigs of yellow dried yarrow
two 1" long sprigs of purple dried larkspur
1" tuft of sheet moss
one ¾" wide wooden watering-can button
one 5" circle of black garden print fabric
one 2"x7" piece of teal cotton fabric
one 1½"x5" piece of natural corrugated paper
dark yellow acrylic paint
4" of lavender #5 perle cotton thread

**1** **Body/head:** Follow step 1 for the snowman, page 86, but substitute the fabric
circle for the batting. Refer to the pattern to
draw the face. **Arms:** Fold the 2"x7" fabric
into thirds lengthwise. Knot the center and
glue the ends behind her neck. **Hair:** Knot
the center of the doll hair, then glue the knot
to the head. Glue the hat to the head as
shown. Glue the moss to the front brim; glue
the flowers into the moss. **Wings:** Trace the
pattern and cut from corrugated paper. Glue
to the angel's back. **Hanger:** Follow step 4 for
the snowman, page 86.

**2** Paint the watering can yellow. Use the
pen to outline it. Insert the lavender
thread through the buttonholes and knot in
front. Glue the watering can to her hands.
Brush on glitter glaze.

wings
(for both angels)

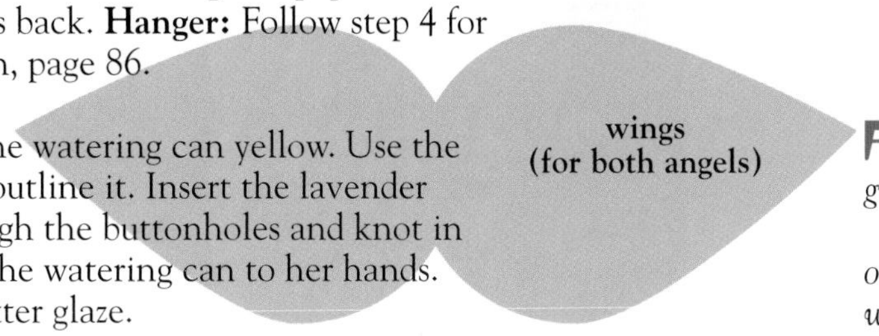

## Scarecrow (center bottom):

six 8" strands of raffia
one 2" wide straw hat
1" tuft of sheet moss
three ½" sprigs of yellow dried yarrow
one ½" wide dark yellow silk flower
orange acrylic paint
one ½" wide green button
two 3" long cinnamon sticks
one 5" circle of brown/black sunflower print fabric
black/ivory checked fabric: one 3"x7" piece, one ½" square

Follow step 1 for the Garden Angel above, substituting the
raffia lengths for the loopy yarn hair. Trim the raffia ends to
1"–1½"; use your fingernail to shred them into thinner
strands. Glue the fabric square to the lower right body; glue
the button to the patch. Glue the cinnamon sticks horizon-
tally to the bottom of the body. Brush on glitter glaze.

each ornament 4" tall

## Peppermint Angel (top right):

green/beige checked flannel fabric: one 5"
    circle, one 3"x7" piece
one 2"x5" piece of natural corrugated paper
wooden cutouts: one ¾" wide star,
    one ¾" circle 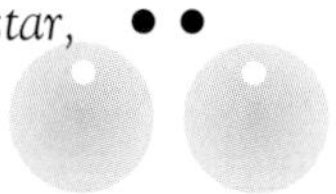
twelve 6" strands of auburn
    lil' Loopies™ doll hair
one 12" stem of green vinyl pine with tinsel

**1** **Halo and wreath:** Cut the pine stem
into two 6" lengths. Wind each into
a 1" circle. Glue one to the back of the
head. Loop the other over her arms before
gluing them on in step 2.

**2** **Body, head, arms, hair, hanger:**
Follow step 1 for the Garden Angel
above, omitting the hat. Paint the star
gold and the wooden circle red. Use the
black pen to draw the detail lines; use the
liner to paint the white details. Glue the
¾" fabric square and the star to the lower
right front. Glue the mint to her hands.
Brush with glitter glaze.

# Llama Ornament

actual height 4¼"

ear

by Sandy Zimmer

dough (see page 142):
    natural, brown
½ paper clip
acrylic paints: black, white
#1 liner paintbrush
polymer sealer
8" of ⅛" wide burgundy
    satin ribbon
aluminum foil
round wooden toothpick
garlic press
low temperature glue gun
    and sticks or tacky craft
    glue

neck

head

eyelid

**1 Body:** Roll a 1½" ball of natural dough and flatten to match the pattern. **Neck:** Roll a ½"x2" rope. Moisten the ends with water and attach to the body; flatten slightly. Attach a ½" ball for the tail.

**2 Head:** Roll a ½" ball of natural dough into an oval with a slightly pointed end. Join to the top of the neck. Roll two ⅛" natural balls into ½" long teardrops and attach for the ears; tip them forward as shown. **Feet:** Roll two ½" natural balls into ovals and flatten slightly. Attach one at the front and one at the back. Roll a ¼" natural ball into an oval and attach above the front leg as shown.

body

**3** Moisten the body and neck area. Fill the garlic press with brown dough. Squeeze out ¼" lengths, lift off with a toothpick and cover the moistened areas. Use ½" lengths to cover the tail.

**4** Roll a ⅛" brown ball for an eye and attach as shown. Roll a ⅛" ball of natural into a ½" long rope and attach over the eye for an eyelid. Insert a paper clip hanger into the back of the head. Bake on foil at 200° until hard (5–6 hours). Let cool. Use the liner brush with black to paint the nose, mouth, eyes and lashes. Use the tip of the liner to paint a white dot in the pupil. Seal; let dry. Use the ribbon to make a shoestring bow (see page 141) with ¾" loops and 1" tails. Glue to the neck.

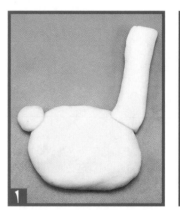

tail

foot

upper leg

# Bear on a Block

### by Barbara McElhaney

dough (see page 142): natural, brown
½ paper clip
1¼" square wooden alphabet block
aluminum foil
acrylic paints: red, white, black
round wooden toothpick
#1 liner paintbrush
polymer sealer
low temperature glue gun and sticks or
    tacky craft glue

head

ear

body

arm
or leg

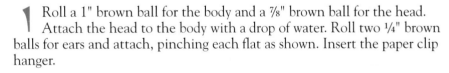 muzzle

actual height 3¼"

**1** Roll a 1" brown ball for the body and a ⅞" brown ball for the head. Attach the head to the body with a drop of water. Roll two ¼" brown balls for ears and attach, pinching each flat as shown. Insert the paper clip hanger.

**2** Roll a ½"x2" brown log and cut into four ½" lengths. Attach as shown. Use your thumb to indent the bottom of each hand and foot. Roll a ¼" brown ball and attach for a tail.

**3** Roll two ⅛" natural balls, flatten and attach for the inner ears. Roll a ⅜" natural ball, flatten and attach for the muzzle. Roll a ⅛" brown ball and attach to the muzzle top for the nose. Roll a a ¼" natural ball and flatten firmly into place for the tummy. Roll four ¼" natural balls, flatten and attach to the feet and hands as shown. Bake on foil at 200° until hard (5–6 hours). Let cool.

**4** Refer to the large photo. Paint black circles for eyes, then use the toothpick to make white dip dots in the pupils. Use the liner to paint black eyebrows and a mouth. Use red to make a tongue and a heart on his tummy. Use the liner to stroke a tiny white highlight on his nose and his heart. Let dry, seal and let dry. Glue the bear to the top of the block.

actual height 5"

# Flossie Doll

### by Marilyn Gossett

*2 skeins of 6-strand ivory embroidery floss*
*¾" wooden bead with a ¼" hole*
*one 4" white scalloped round crocheted doily*
*½ yard of ⅛" wide beige satin ribbon*
*9" of thin gold cord*
*three ⅜" wide ivory satin ribbon roses with green leaves*
*⅝" wide wicker basket with a ⅜" tall handle*
*pink powdered blush, cotton swab, black fine-tip permanent pen*
*cellophane tape, needle, white thread*
*low temperature glue gun and sticks or tacky craft glue*

**1** Remove the floss skeins from the paper wrapping and lay them side by side. Cut the loops at both ends and trim to 6" long. Save three strands and set aside for step 2. Tightly tape one end of the remaining strands, twist and push them up through the bead until 2" extends and remove the tape. Pull twelve 2" strands over the face and trim for bangs.

**2** Drape the 2" of floss evenly around the head for hair, gluing as needed to secure. **Arms:** Separate ¼ of the lower strands on each side. Twist each arm away from you and tie 2" below the head with a reserved strand. Trim ½" below the tie. Tie the last reserved strand around her waist ½" below the head.

**3** **Dress:** Fold the scallops down ¾" on the top of the doily. Sew a running stitch ⅛" below the fold and gather to 1" wide. Glue to the front of the doll. Wrap the sides to the back and glue. Wrap 9" of ribbon around the waist and tie in front, making a shoestring bow (see page 141) with ½" loops and 3" tails.

**4** Knot the ends of the gold cord and glue to the back of the doll's head. Glue the roses into the basket, slip the handle over her arms and glue her hands together. Cut the remaining ribbon in half and use each length to make a shoestring bow with ¼" loops and ¼" tails. Glue one to the basket front and the other to the top of her head.

1

2

3

back view

4

# Abaca Angel Ornament

by Paula M. Cornec

4" wide natural abaca fan
one 20mm wooden bead with a ⅛" wide hole
½ yard of ⅝" wide ivory satin ribbon
15" of ⅛" wide mauve satin ribbon
two ⅜" wide mauve ribbon roses with green leaves
6" length of thin gold cord (hanger)
acrylic paints: black, white, mauve
paintbrushes: #4 flat, #1 liner
tracing paper, pencil, transfer paper
low temperature glue gun and sticks or tacky craft glue

**actual height 4¾"**

**1** Transfer (see page 143) the face to one side of the bead. Use the flat brush to paint wispy black hair, and the brush handle to dip dot black eyes. Let dry. Use the liner brush to dot white highlights in the eyes and a mauve mouth; let dry. Fold the fan into a cone, overlapping ¾" at the back, and glue. Insert the loop of the fan through the bead and glue to secure.

**2** **Hands:** Cut a 6" length of ivory ribbon and knot the center. Glue the ribbon ends to the back just below the head as shown.

**3** **Wings:** Use the remaining ivory ribbon to make a loopy bow (see page 140) with four 1½" loops and no tails. Glue the bow to the back of her shoulders. Use 9" of mauve ribbon to make a shoestring bow with ¾" loops and 3" tails. Glue to the center of the ivory bow. Glue a rose to the bow center.

**4** Use the remaining mauve ribbon to make a shoestring bow (see page 141) with ½" loops and ½" tails; glue to the angel's neck. Glue a rose to her hands. Thread the gold cord through the fan loop and knot the ends for a hanger.

**back view**

# Rudy Reindeer

by Joann Pearson

one 6" long brown mini straw broom
two 15mm round wiggle eyes
one pair of ½" long novelty eyelashes
two 1" wide brown pom poms
one ½" wide red pom pom
1 yard of ¼" wide green satin ribbon
½" square of red felt
30-gauge wire
low temperature glue gun and sticks or tacky craft glue

 tongue

back view

**1** Turn the broom upside down. Divide the bristles into two equal bunches and wrap the ends tightly with wire, ½" below the top. Trim the wire ends. Cut two 9" ribbon lengths and tie one over the wire on each side, making a shoestring bow (see page 140) with ¾" loops and 1" tails.

**2** Glue the brown pom poms for the muzzle and the red pom pom for his nose.

**3** Glue the eyes as shown. Glue eyelashes around the top of each eye. Trace the tongue pattern and cut from red felt. Glue under the muzzle as shown.

**4** Use a 9" ribbon length of ribbon to tie a shoestring bow with 1" loops and 1½" tails. Glue the bow below his chin. Fold a 4" ribbon length into a loop and glue the ends to the back of the ornament as shown for a hanger.

# Pom Pom Bear in Santa's Hat by Teresa Nelson

4" square of red felt
twelve ½" wide white pom poms (hat trim)
tan pom poms: two 1" wide, four ½" wide,
    three ¼" wide
two 3mm half-round beads
one 4mm round bead
two ½" wide gold or silver foil packages
one ⅝" wide gold star charm
9" of ⅛" wide green satin ribbon
9" of thin gold cord
tracing paper, pencil
low temperature glue gun and sticks or tacky
    craft glue

actual height 4"

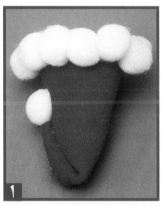

1 Trace the hat pattern and cut one from red felt. Form it into a cone and glue the straight sides together. Turn it upside down and glue eleven white pom poms around the brim. Bend the hat tip up, glue to secure, then glue the last white pom pom to the tip.

2 Glue the 1" tan pom poms together to make the body and head. Glue the ½" pom poms onto the body for the arms and legs. Glue one ¼" pom pom to the face for a muzzle and the others for ears.

3 Glue the 4mm bead for the nose and the half-round beads for eyes. Use the ribbon to make a shoestring bow (see page 141) with ½" loops and ½" tails. Glue the bow under the bear's chin, then tuck the bear into the hat and glue to secure.

4 Glue the packages between his hands and the star onto one paw. Tie the ends of the gold cord together to make a loop, part the pom pom at the top of his head and glue the knot in to make a hanger.

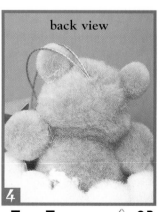

back view

actual height 5"

# Stocking Ornament

### by Marilyn Gossett

*green plaid cotton fabric: one ¾"x1" piece, one 2½"x1" piece*
*red plaid cotton fabric: one ¾"x1" piece, one 1"x10" piece, two ½"x2½" pieces*
*5"x8" piece of cotton batting*
*one 3" long cinnamon stick*
*two ¾" wide wooden star buttons*
*two 1" tall wooden gingerbread man buttons*
*#5 green perle cotton thread, needle*
*acrylic paints: brown, dark yellow, white, red*
*brush-on glitter glaze*
*#4 flat paintbrush*
*round wooden toothpick*
*tracing paper, pencil*
*low temperature glue gun and sticks or tacky craft glue*

stocking

**1 Stocking:** Trace the pattern and cut two stockings from cotton batting. Glue the 2½" strip of green plaid fabric to one stocking top—fold the edge and ends to the back. Place the two stockings together and sew a blanket stitch (see page 144) around the sides and bottom. Glue the ¾"x1 patches to the stocking front as shown.

**2 Hanger:** Fold each ½"x2½" red fabric piece into a loop, right sides out; glue the ends together. Glue the loops 1" apart to the stocking back with the tops extending ¾" above the stocking. Thread the cinnamon stick through the loops. Tie a 10" thread length to the ends of the cinnamon stick for a hanger. **Bow:** Use the 1"x10" red fabric strip to tie a shoestring bow (see page 141) with

¾" loops and 2½" tails. Cut the tails diagonally. Glue the bow to the right end of the cinnamon stick.

**3 Buttons:** Paint the stars yellow. Paint the gingerbread men brown. Use a toothpick to apply red and white dip dots (see page 143). Use the black pen to draw the eyes and mouth.

**4** Cut four 6" thread lengths. Insert one through the holes of each button and knot in the front. Trim the ends to ½". Glue the stars to the stocking top and a gingerbread man to each patch. Use the pen to draw stitch lines around the outsides of the patches. Brush glitter lightly over the entire stocking.

# Frosty Fellow

by Rita Smith

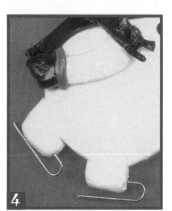

polymer clay: white, black,
  orange, purple, green
one 1½" long eye pin
two 1" long paper clips
wire cutters
two 3mm black half-round
  beads
gloss acrylic varnish
ultra fine iridescent glitter
pink powdered blush
cotton swab
X-acto® knife or sharp knife
darning needle
tracing paper, pencil
rolling pin
baking sheet, oven

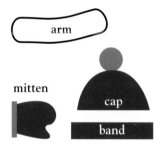

arm

mitten

cap

band

**actual height 2⅝"**

**1** Trace and cut out the patterns. Roll a 1¼" ball of white clay to ¼" thick. Cut one body, one of each leg and one head. Smooth all edges. Press the head and legs onto the body as shown. **Arms:** Roll a ¼"x2" white log; cut in half. Flatten each slightly, curve, and attach as shown, one on the front and one on the back. Flatten the top of each arm and smooth it into the shoulder.

body

**2** Flatten a 1" purple ball to ¼" thick. Cut two mittens and one cap. Attach the cap to the back of his head and a mitten to the end of each arm. Roll the purple clay to ¹⁄₁₆" thick. Cut a ¼"x3" strip and press it around the bottom of the hat, slightly overlapping the seam. Trim any excess clay. Use the needle to draw lines on the cap and hatband as shown. **Scarf:** Cut a strip ¼"x4" strip of purple clay. Make three ¼" cuts at each end of the scarf for fringe. Wrap it around his neck, crossing the ends at the shoulder.

**3** Press a ¼" green ball onto the cap top for a pom pom. Make a ⅛" L-shaped bend at the bottom of the eye pin. Insert into the top of his head, then rotate it a half turn to secure it. **Face:** Roll a ⅛"x⅜" orange cone and attach close to the edge of his face, angling to the right as shown. Press in the beads for eyes. Roll five teeny-tiny black balls (¹⁄₃₂") and attach in a curved line below his nose. Roll three ¹⁄₁₆" black balls and flatten onto the right edge of his chest for buttons.

**4** Roll a ¹⁄₁₆"x2" green rope and cut in half. Wrap one around each wrist. Cut the paper clips as shown in the diagram. Insert the short end of one into the bottom of each leg. Bake at 265° for 30 minutes, let cool and remove from the oven. Blush his cheeks. Varnish all the colored areas; let dry. Varnish the white areas and while the varnish is wet dust lightly with glitter. Let dry.

actual height 4¼"

# Snowman Ornament

**by Nancy Overmyer**

*dough (see page 142): white, green*
*acrylic paints: black, green, white,*
    *red, orange*
*#1 liner paintbrush*
*pink powdered blush, cotton swab*
*1 ¼"x1 ½" piece of aluminum can*
    *(cut carefully with tin snips or*
    *heavy-duty scissors)*
*½ paper clip*
*round wooden toothpick, bamboo*
    *skewer, aluminum foil, polymer*
    *sealer*
*X-acto® knife or sharp knife*
*low temperature glue gun and sticks*
    *or tacky craft glue*

**nose**

**head**

**arm**

**scarf**

**body**

**1**

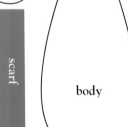
**2**

**1** Roll a 1½" ball of white into a 2" tall pointed oval and flatten slightly. Flatten a ¾" ball to 1" across, moisten with water and attach for a head. Roll a ¼" ball of white into a cone and attach for his nose.

**2** Roll a ¾" ball of white, flatten one side to form a cone and attach to the top of the head for a cap. Roll a ¼"x1½" green rope and wrap around the cap for a brim. Roll a ⅛" green ball and attach to the top for a pom pom.

**3** Roll two ¾" white balls into 1½" long teardrops and attach the pointed ends to his shoulders. Wrap his right hand over his tummy and extend the left to the side. Flatten two ¼"x1½" green ropes to ½" across. Use a knife to cut fringe lines in the ends. Drape one over his left shoulder and down his tummy, the other around his neck. Insert the paper clip hanger into the cap top. Bake at 200° until hard (4–5 hours).

**4** Use the toothpick to dip dot (see page 143) black eyes and a mouth. Paint his nose orange. Use the brush handle and a toothpick to make green dip dots of various sizes on his hat and white ones on the scarf. Seal and let dry. Paint the skewer red. Glue the aluminum on the end of the skewer, then glue it into the snowman's hands.

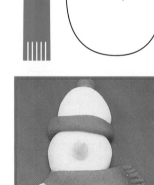
**3**

**4**

**cap**

# Polar Bear Ornaments

**by Nancy Overmyer**

head

body

leg

paw

*for each bear:*
white dough (see page 142)
acrylic paints: coral, black
#1 liner paintbrush, pink powdered blush, cotton swab
round wooden toothpick, aluminum foil, polymer sealer
X-acto® knife or sharp knife, ½ paper clip
low temperature glue gun and sticks or tacky craft glue

*for the fish bear:*
wooden cutouts: two 1″ long ovals, two ¾″ wide triangles
acrylic paints: brown, peach, white, green
6″ of jute twine

*for the wreath bear:*
6″ of 1″ wide pine garland, five ¼″ wide artificial red berries

**1** Flatten a 1½″ ball of white into a 2¼″ tall pear. Roll two ½″x1½″ white logs, moisten with water, and attach side by side at the center bottom of the body.

**2** Roll two ¾″ white balls for back feet and two ½″ white balls for front feet. Flatten slightly and use the knife to score toe lines. Moisten the back feet and attach at his lower sides. Moisten the front feet and attach at the bottoms of the legs, slightly overlapping the back feet.

**3** **Head:** Flatten a 1″ white ball into an oval. Use the knife to score a muzzle line at the bottom. Pinch a ⅛″ white ball into a triangle and place at the top of the line for a nose. Roll two ⅛″ white balls for ears. Attach at the top back of his head; indent with the paintbrush handle. Insert the paper clip hanger into the top of the head.

**4** Bake at 200° until hard (4–5 hours). Let cool. Use the toothpick to dip dot (see page 143) black eyes. Paint the inner ears coral and the nose black. Blush his cheeks. Seal; let dry. **Fish bear:** Knot the jute ends together. Glue the knot to the back of his neck and the bottom of the loop to his tummy. Fish: Glue a triangle to the back of each

each ornament
3½″ tall

oval. Paint one fish green and one brown. Dip dot white eyes. Use the liner to paint white fin lines and scales on the green fish. Paint coral fin lines on the brown fish and dip dot coral scales. Glue to the jute. **Wreath bear:** Refer to the large photo. Form the garland into a circle, glue it around his neck and glue the berries evenly spaced to the front.

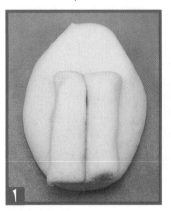

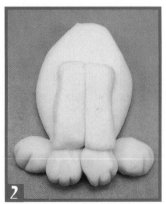

# Wrap It Up!

Remember the excitement on Christmas morning of viewing all the beautifully wrapped presents around the tree, just waiting for you to discover the treasures they held? Of course, we thought the wrappings were simply there to disguise the gift—something to tear away to reveal the much-desired present we'd asked Santa to deliver.

Well, we've created wrappings you won't want to remove from the gifts. In fact, many of them are actually part of the gift itself! Beautiful Bottles shown on pages 102–103 are decorated with gilded trims and ribbons; fill them with fragrant bath salts and you've created a very unique gift tailored to a special friend.

We've also supplied options for making a plain bag into something wonderful. Whether it's a fabric bag constructed with simple sewing or a paper bag that's decorated with paints, fabrics and trims, we have just the size, shape and theme to cover that hard-to-wrap gift.

We decorated trinket boxes, terra cotta pots, bottles, bags and papier-mâché boxes—everything we could dream of to help you make your Christmas gifts distinctive and unusual. We hope you enjoy this collection of sensational wrappings!

# A BEVY OF BAGS by LeNae Gerig

To make a basic fabric bag, just fold the fabric in half, right sides together, and sew two sides (the fold will be the third side). Turn the bag right side out, press the seams, place your gift inside and tie the top closed with ribbon or cord. You can make an infinite variety of bags just by changing the size, shape and fabric.

## HOLLY BAG

Use a 9"x18" piece of holly print fabric or another Christmas fabric folded crosswise to make this bag. Wrap 1 yard of burgundy cord three times around the bag neck. Tie in a shoestring bow (see page 141), knot 1" from each end of the cord and fray the ends. For a sparkling touch, use thread or a strand of the cord to tie on a small bell.

## MITTEN BAG

This taller bag is made from an 8"x30" fabric strip folded crosswise. For a rustic look, the seams were sewn wrong sides together, leaving the raw edges visible on the outside. For the gift tag: Trace the pattern onto a 2½" foam square, cut out and glue on a ½"x2" strip of contrasting color for the cuff. Use a paper punch to make a hole in the corner. Hold several strands of raffia together and insert through the hole before tying it around the bag neck.

## STRIPED BAG

To make a bag with a country theme use striped fabric in soft colors (to make the stripes run vertically, the 18"x10" fabric piece was sewn along the bottom and one side, rather than on opposite sides). Tie two 18" lengths of jute twine around the bag neck in a shoestring bow (see page 141) and knot the tails. A wooden heart with a jute hanger makes a clever tag: Use a gold paint pen to write "Merry Christmas" and tie it around the neck. To complement the country look, insert sprigs of wheat heads behind the bow.

## BURLAP BAG

Iron 2"–3" squares of paper-backed fusible web onto scraps of cotton fabric, cut out and iron them onto a 10"x18" piece of burlap. Sew as for the striped bag above. Glue on buttons, then tear a 1"x18" long strip of matching fabric for the tie.

## FELT SNOWMAN BAG

*two 9"x12" pieces of navy blue felt*
*3"x6" piece of white felt*
*3"x3" piece of black felt*
*12" of ¼" wide green satin ribbon*
*two ½" wide burgundy heart buttons*
*two 2" long twigs*
*dimensional paints: black, orange, clear glitter, gold*
*powdered blush, cotton swab*
*sewing machine, white thread*
*tracing paper, pencil*
*low temperature glue gun and sticks or tacky craft glue*

**1** Sew the 9"x12" felt pieces together with a ¼"
seam, leaving the top open. Trace the snowman
patterns; cut one head and one body from white felt.
Cut the hat, brim and boots from black felt. Glue the
pieces to the bag as shown.

**2** Use black paint to squeeze dots for the eyes and
mouth. Squeeze orange for the nose. Blush the
cheeks. Glue the buttons and twig arms as shown. Use
dots of clear glitter paint all over the bag to represent
falling snow. Use gold paint to personalize the bag.

**3** With the ribbon, tie a shoestring bow (see page
141) with ⅝" loops and ⅝" tails; glue to his neck.
Glue the remaining ribbon for the hatband.

## GUEST TOWEL BAG

*one 12"x22" ivory battenburg guest towel*
*2¼" wide gold heart charm*
*12" of ¼" wide white satin ribbon*
*1 yard of white tulle net*
*sewing machine, ivory thread*

Fold the towel in half, right sides together, and sew the
sides together with ¼" seams. Turn right side out; iron
the seams. Thread the ribbon through the charm and
tie to the lace at the bag front. Wrap your gift in the
tulle and place it in the bag.

## CHAMPAGNE BOTTLE BAG

*bottle of champagne*
*7½"x 33" piece of burgundy cotton fabric (or measure the*
  *diameter of your bottle and add 1½", then measure the*
  *length and add 2" to get the proper size)*
*⅔ yard of 3" wide sheer gold wire-edged ribbon*
*3" long gold holly charm*
*sewing machine, burgundy thread*
*low temperature glue gun and sticks or tacky craft glue*

Fold the fabric right sides together and sew the sides
with ¼" seams. Turn right side out, fold the top down
3" inside the bag, iron and glue to secure. Place the bottle in the bag. Gather the bag around the bottle neck
and tie with the ribbon, making a shoestring bow (see
page 141) with 2½" loops and 8" tails. Glue the charm
below the bow center.

hat

hat brim

boot

# BEAUTIFUL BOTTLES

## BOTTLE WITH OVAL MEDALLION

by Marilyn Gossett

*one 2⅜"x5"x2" triangular clear green glass bottle with cork*
*one 2"x2¾" self-adhesive foam oval*
*one 3"x4" rectangle of ivory moiré taffeta fabric*
*8" of ½" wide green/metallic gold flat braid*
*7" of ¼" burgundy flat rose braid*
*21" of ⅛" wide burgundy rope braid*
*15" of ⅜" wide green satin picot ribbon*
*one 1" wide brass heart charm*
*low temperature glue gun and sticks or tacky craft glue*

Press the fabric onto the foam oval, pulling the edges firmly to the back to create a slightly domed oval. Glue ½" braid along the center of the oval, turning the ends to the back. Glue a row of rose braid ¼" away on each side of the green braid. Glue the oval to one side of the bottle. Glue rope braid around the outside edge of the oval. Tie the ribbon around the neck in a shoestring bow (see page 141) with 1" loops and 2½" tails. Glue the remaining rope braid around the cork top in a flat spiral, tucking the end under. Glue the remaining ½" braid trim around the sides of the cork. Glue the charm to the top.

## GOLD/IVORY BOTTLE

by LeNae Gerig

*3"x4"x1½" clear green glass bottle with cork*
*1½" wide wooden knob with a flat side*
*1" square of kitchen sponge*
*gold acrylic paint*
*paper towels*
*matte acrylic spray sealer*
*#8 flat paintbrush*
*1 yard of ⅛" wide gold/ivory rope braid*
*1 yard of heavy gold thread*
*three 6mm white pearls*
*1¼" round brass Santa charm*
*one 3½" long sprig of preserved plumosus*
*scented bath oil or water*

Remove the cork, spray the bottle with sealer and let dry. Moisten the sponge, dip into gold paint, blot on a paper towel and lightly sponge all over the bottle. Let dry. Paint the cork and the knob gold; let dry. Glue the knob to the top of the cork. Place the plumosus sprig in the bottle, fill with liquid and replace the cork.

Use the rope braid to make a loopy bow (see page 140) with four 1" loops and 2½" tails. Glue to the bottle neck. Cut the gold thread in half, hold both lengths together and handle as one to make a loopy bow with six 1" loops and 2"–3" tails. Glue to the center of the rope braid bow. Glue the pearls to the center of the bows and the charm to the bottle side just below the bow center.

# BURGUNDY & GREEN BOTTLE

by Marilyn Gossett

one 2½"x3"x1½" hexagonal green glass bottle with cork
one 1" wide gold heart charm
one ½" wide gold filigree button
15" of ¼" wide burgundy flat rose braid
6" of ½" wide green scalloped flat braid
12" of ⅜" wide burgundy satin ribbon
low temperature glue gun and sticks or tacky craft glue

Glue the charm to the top front of the bottle. Wrap the ribbon around the bottle neck and tie in a shoestring bow (see page 141) with 1" loops and 1½" tails. Glue the green braid around the top of the cork—be careful to leave enough space at the bottom to insert the cork into the bottle. Glue the rose braid in a flat spiral, overlapping the wraps slightly and tucking the end under. Glue the button to the center of the braid (see inset).

top view

# PAINTED BOTTLE WITH GOLD ROSE

by Marilyn Gossett

one 1¾"x4½"x1¾" square glass bottle with cork
24" of ¾" wide silver/gold flat braid
18" of ¼" wide silver/gold flat braid
acrylic paints: green, ivory
matte acrylic spray sealer
1" sponge brush
1" square of kitchen sponge
one 1" wide gold metallic ribbon rose
low temperature glue gun and sticks or tacky craft glue

Remove the cork from the bottle. Seal the bottle and let dry. Paint the cork and the bottle green. Dip the sponge in ivory paint and dab it lightly over the bottle to create a marbled effect. Glue the end of the ¾" trim inside the bottle rim above the center of one flat side. Glue the trim down the center, under the bottom of the bottle and up the center of the opposite side; trim excess and glue the trim end into the rim. Repeat in the other direction. Glue ¼" trim around the top of the cork; trim excess. Glue the remaining trim around the bottle neck, knotting in the front. Trim each tail diagonally to 2½". Glue the ribbon rose to the knot. Replace the cork.

# CHRISTMAS TREE BAG

by Tracia Ledford

*7"x8" papier-mâché bag with handles*
*acrylic paints: red, yellow, green, brown*
*3"x6" piece of compressed sponge*
*paper plate, paper towels*
*tracing paper, pencil*

1 Trace the patterns and cut from the compressed sponge. Dip in water to expand the shapes; wring out excess water. Pour a 2" puddle of red paint onto a paper plate, dip in the 2" square sponge and dab excess paint onto a paper towel. Sponge the color lightly over the entire bag, letting the natural color show through. Let dry.

2 Dip the triangular sponge into green and sponge three trees onto the bag front in a row as shown; repeat on the back. Use the small rectangular sponge with brown to make the trunks. Use the star sponge with yellow to make a star on top of each tree. Sponge random stars over the bag sides. Let dry.

2" square

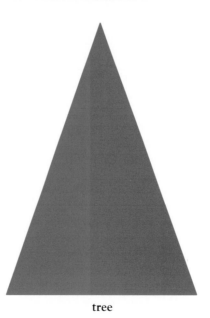

tree

trunk

star

# BROWN PAPER GIFT BAGS
by LeNae Gerig

*for each bag:* ¼" hole punch
*for the bag with horn:*
one 13" tall brown paper bag
spray webbing: gold, mauve
18" of ⅛" wide burgundy satin
  ribbon
18" of ¼" wide mauve satin ribbon
4" long gold plastic French horn
36" of heavy gold thread
newspapers

Open the bag and set it on the
newspapers. Lightly spray with
mauve, then gold webbing; let dry.
Fold the top of the bag down 2½"
and punch two holes ½" apart ½"
from the fold. Insert the gift. Cut
the thread in half. Hold the ribbon
and thread lengths together and
handle as one. Thread through the holes and tie around the
horn in a shoestring bow (see page 141) with 2" loops and
3"–5" tails. Knot the end of each tail.

*for the star bag:*
9" tall brown paper bag
1½" square of compressed sponge
acrylic paints: yellow, white
two 12" strands of raffia
black fine-tip permanent pen
tracing paper, pencil, old toothbrush, newspapers

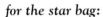

Open the bag and set it on the newspapers. Trace the star
pattern and cut from the compressed sponge. Moisten with
water and dip into yellow paint, blot excess paint on the
newspapers and sponge randomly over the bag; let dry. Use
the pen to outline each star with stitch marks. Dip the
toothbrush into water, then into white paint. Pull the bristles back with your thumb to spatter the bag; let dry. Insert
the gift. Fold the top of the bag down 1½" and punch two
holes ½" apart ½" from the fold. Thread raffia through the
holes and tie in a shoestring bow (see page 141) with 2"
loops and 5" tails.

*for the heart and patches bag:*
9" tall brown paper bag
12" of jute twine
one 1¾"x2¾" wooden heart
buttons: one ½" wide burgundy heart, one ¾" round green
fabric, torn with ragged edges: 1½"x2" piece of burgundy/
  white print, 3" square of burgundy/navy check
black fine-tip permanent pen
acrylic paints: dark green, white
paintbrushes: #4 flat, #1 liner
low temperature glue gun and sticks or tacky craft glue

Glue the fabric pieces to the bag front as shown. Paint the
wooden heart green and use the liner brush with white
paint to write "Love" on it. Glue the heart and buttons to
the fabric as shown. Use the pen to outline the fabric with
stitch marks. Insert the gift. Fold the top of the bag down
1½" and punch two holes ½" apart ½" from the fold.
Thread the jute through the holes and tie in a shoestring
bow (see page 141) with 1¼" loops and 2½" tails.

*for the stocking bag:*
9" tall brown paper bag
4½"x6" piece of red fabric printed with white hearts
3" square of white fabric printed with red hearts
tracing paper, pencil, paper-backed fusible web, iron
¾" wide wooden star
green acrylic paint, #4 flat paintbrush                    **cuff**
white dimensional paint
low temperature glue gun and sticks or tacky craft glue

Tear a 1"x6" strip of red fabric and set aside. Iron web onto
the wrong side of both remaining fabric pieces. Trace the
patterns. Cut a stocking from red fabric with a cuff, heel
and toe from white. Fuse the stocking to the front of the
bag, then fuse the cuff, toe and heel to the stocking. Paint
the star green; squeeze white paint dots; let dry. Glue the
star to the top right of the stocking. Insert the gift. Fold the
top of the bag down 1½" and punch two holes ½" apart ½"
from the fold. Thread the remaining red fabric strip
through the holes and knot.

**toe**          **heel**

# CREATIVE WRAP-UPS

by Anne-Marie Spencer

Once you've finished all your holiday crafting you're ready to undertake what for many is the biggest challenge of the holiday season—wrapping the gifts! You could buy the same printed rolls of paper and pre-made bows again, but WAIT! Why not make your gift wrap as creative as the item inside?

The four elegant gift wraps on this page and the next each began with a roll of white butcher paper. The package decorations were all left over from other craft projects: odd picks, a loose flower from a stem, wooden stars. What a great way to clean out that "bits and pieces" drawer!

## GOLD DOTS

The gold polka-dot package below is simply wrapped once in each direction with sheer gold-dotted 5" wide ribbon. A similar but narrower (1¼" wide) ribbon is used for the puffy bow, and the package is tied with a fuzzy gold metallic cord. The bow is decorated with sprigs of preserved plumosus and a 1" wide gold-sprayed silk rose.

## GOLD TASSELS & CONES

The paper for this gold package is cut to size, then sprayed with gold metallic paint. A gold mesh ribbon is used for the ties and loopy bow. Streamers of fine gold tinsel hang below the bow, which is easily embellished with a glittery Christmas pick.

## HOLLY & RIBBON

A leftover Christmas pick with copper leaves, burgundy berries and a burgundy foil package provides the color inspiration for this elegantly wrapped gift. The paper is spatter-painted with copper metallic paint. Burgundy moiré taffeta ribbon is used for the tie and puffy bow.

## CELESTIAL GOLD

The paper for this "heavenly" package is cut to size and lightly spritzed with navy blue spray paint, then with gold. A 1" star cut from a compressed sponge (see page 104) is used to print evenly spaced navy stars on the paper. Once the navy stars are dry, sponge gold metallic stars over them for a three-dimensional effect. The package is tied with gold cord over ½" wide navy ribbon, then the same gold cord is used for the loopy bow. A black permanent pen is used to letter "Merry Christmas" on a 1½" gold-painted wooden star to decorate the bow center. Other ¾"–1" gold and navy stars are glued to the bow tails.

## GIFT TAGS

Matching gift tags can be cut from scraps of your decorated paper— 4"x2" is a nice size. Fold to 2" square and write your message on the plain inside. Embellish with matching ribbon (see the gold package on page 106), floral sprigs, wooden cutouts or stickers.

# CINNAMON-COVERED BOX

*one 8″ square papier-mâché box with lid*
*cinnamon sticks: four 8″ long, about forty-two 4″ long, about eighty 3″ long*
*2 yards of 1″ wide rust woven paper ribbon*
*three 1″ long pine cones*
*handful of green sheet moss*
*low temperature glue gun and sticks or tacky craft glue*

**A papier-mâché box decorated with cinnamon sticks makes a fragrant, reusable container for homemade Christmas cookies or candies.**

1 Glue 8″ cinnamon sticks around the bottom edge of the box. Glue the 3″ sticks vertically around the sides as shown in the photo above.

2 Section the box lid into quarters. Glue 4″ cinnamon sticks to fill each section, alternating the directions as shown. Glue the ribbon around the sides of the lid.

3 Use the remaining ribbon to make a puffy bow (see page 141) with six 3″ loops. Glue to the center of the lid; glue the cones to the bow center.

4 Glue moss around the cones. Use the edge of a knife blade to poke moss into any openings between cinnamon sticks where the box shows through.

# RAFFIA & CEDAR
## (SHOWN ON PAGE 108)

Shredded raffia fastens the brown paper package on page 108, with long raffia tails left to hang loose. A "bow" of crossed 8" cinnamon sticks and preserved cedar is decorated with dried red berries and alder cones. The 2" square tag is made of folded corrugated paper, also embellished with berries, cedar and a 1½" length of cinnamon stick.

# FRIENDLY FISH

This wrap to delight a fisherman's heart features a sea grass rope for the ties and shoestring bow over brown paper. Dried cedar sprigs, cones and wheat heads adorn the bow, but the real focus is the primitive hand-carved and painted fish ornaments glued to the bow tails.

# CORRUGATED WRAP

Here a "tie" of 1" wide birch bark secures a wrapping of corrugated paper. A tuft of dried sheet moss makes a nest for a mushroom bird. Sprigs of cedar, dried twigs and pods add to the rustic look. The gift tag, of matching corrugated paper, is tied with jute twine and decorated with a birch bark square and a moss tuft.

# TEACHER GIFT BAG & CARD

### by Marilyn Gossett

**for each project:**
one 5″ square of 140# watercolor
    paper
watercolor paints: green, brown, red
#4 flat paintbrush
tracing paper, pencil
black and white transfer paper
low temperature glue gun and sticks or
    tacky craft glue

**for the bag:**
one 8″x10½″ black paper bag with
    handles
1 yard of ¼″ wide dark green
    curly ribbon
black fine-tip permanent pen
white paint pen
⅛″ hole punch

**for the card:**
5″x6″ white plain greeting card with
    envelope
fine-tip green permanent pen
decorative edge scissors

1 **Apple:** Transfer (see page 143) the pattern to the paper. Wet the brush and dab water inside the apple outline. Apply red paint to the brush and blend. Brush the red paint around the outside edges of the apple. Add more water to the paint to lighten the color as you work toward the center. Use the same technique to paint the leaves green and the stem brown. Blend a tiny bit of green water color around the edge of the apple; let dry.

2 **Bag:** Use the black pen to draw a line-dot pattern (— • — •) around the outside edges of the apple, stem and leaves. Write "Teachers are Special" across the top of the apple. Cut out the apple. Punch two holes ½″ apart below the stem. Tie the ribbon through the

holes, knot and curl by pulling the ribbon across a scissors blade. Use your fingernail to split the curled ribbon into narrower strands.

3 Glue the apple to the bag. Use the white pen to draw a line-dot pattern around the bag edges. Write "Aa Bb Cc," "CAT," "DOG," "Special Teacher," and the sums on the bag as shown. Transfer the cat and go over the lines with the white pen.

4 **Card:** Use decorative scissors to cut out the apple. Glue it to the center front of the card. Use the green pen to write "A+ Teacher" around the apple and to draw curly tendrils above the leaves.

# CARDS & SHRINK PLASTIC ORNAMENTS

plastic heart for teacher card

by **Marilyn Gossett**

*basic supplies:*
shrink plastic (one sheet will do several ornaments)
fine sandpaper, sharp scissors, ⅛" hole punch
paintbrushes: # round, #2 flat
black fine-tip permanent pen
oven, non-stick baking sheet
low temperature glue gun and sticks or tacky craft glue

*for each ornament:*
4" of gold elastic thread
one ⅜" gold jump ring

angel's flower

*for each card:*
one 5x6½" white plain card with envelope
decorative edge scissors
transparent tape

*for the angel ornament:*
acrylic paints: white, pink, pale peach, blue, green
brush-on glitter glaze

angel wings

*for the angel card:*
1" square of household sponge
blue acrylic paint, tracing paper, pencil

banner
(pink for angel;
white for teacher)

*or the teacher ornament:*
acrylic paints: white, green, red, black, pale beach, brown, pink

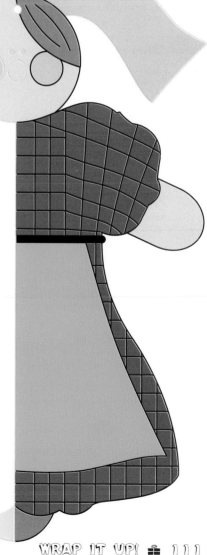

1. Lightly sand the plastic so the paint will adhere better. Place it over the chosen pattern and trace the lines (some are shown in gray) with the pen. Turn the pieces over and paint the back as shown on the pattern; use a blend of three parts water to one part paint (the colors will be pale). Cut out the pieces. Punch a hole at the top of the head. Preheat the oven to 250°–275°. Place the cut pieces on the baking sheet in the oven. Watch carefully. As the plastic shrinks it will curl, then flatten again. When it is flat (in about a minute) remove from the oven. Glue the jump ring to the back of her head for a halo (be careful not to cover the hole).

2. **Angel ornament:** After baking, brush glitter onto her dress. Dip dot (see page 143) three pink buttons on the front. Glue the wings to her back, the flower to the banner and the banner into her hands. **Card:** Trace the heart and use decorative scissors to cut it out. Lay it on the card front, sponge blue paint around the outside, discard the paper heart and let dry. Write "Peace on Earth…Peace on Earth…Peace on Earth…" around the inside of the sponged area. Follow step 3 to attach the angel to the card.

paper heart for angel card

3. **Teacher ornament:** Dip dot two white buttons onto her bodice. Glue the banner into her hands and the heart to her back for wings. Insert one end of the gold cord through the hole, even the ends and knot close to the top of her head; knot the ends together. **Card:** Write "Merry Christmas" on the top front of the card and "— • #1 Teacher — • — • #1 Teacher" repeated along the right edge of the INSIDE card. Use decorative scissors to trim away the right edge of the card front. Make dash-and-dot lines around the front edges. Position the teacher on the card front and cut a ½"–1" slit above her halo. Insert the knotted end of the hanger through the slit and tape the knot inside the card. Repeat the dot-and-dash pattern to outline the ornament.

# TERRA COTTA GIFT POTS

by Marilyn Gossett

**for each pot:**
*one 3½" wide terra cotta pot*
*metallic gold acrylic paint*
*1" sponge brush*
*1" square of household sponge*
*fine sandpaper, matte acrylic sealer*
*generous handful of excelsior*
*low temperature glue gun and sticks or tacky craft glue*

**for the ivory pot:**
*ivory acrylic paint*
*one ¾" wide brass basket charm*
*12" of ⅝" wide metallic gold/ivory flat braid*
*1¼ yards of ½" wide ivory scalloped flat braid*
*½ yard of ⅛" wide ivory rope braid*

**for the green pot:**
*green acrylic paint*
*1¼ yards of ⅜" wide gold metallic flat braid*
*20" of ¾" wide metallic red/gold flat braid*
*12" of ¼" wide flat gold braid with ½" gold loops along one edge*

1 Lightly sand the pot to remove any rough edges. Coat inside and out with sealer; let dry. **Ivory pot:** Use the sponge brush to paint the pot ivory, inside and out; let dry. Moisten the sponge, dip in metallic gold paint and dab it lightly over the entire surface, letting the ivory show through. Let dry.

2 Cut eight 5" lengths of scalloped braid. Glue 1" of one end inside the pot rim. Wrap and glue it down the side; trim the end even with the bottom. Repeat with the remaining lengths, spacing them evenly around the pot. Glue the ends of the remaining scalloped braid to the inside of the pot to form the handle—for security, the braid ends should be glued down all the way to the bottom of the pot.

3 Glue the gold/ivory braid around the rim of the pot with the loops extending slightly above the rim. Glue two rows of rope braid around the pot bottom. Glue the charm to the pot front as shown. Fill the pot with excelsior and place a gift inside.

4 **Green pot:** Follow steps 1–2, substituting green paint for ivory and the ⅜" gold braid for the scalloped braid. Glue the loopy braid around the rim so the loops extend above the rim. Glue red/gold braid around the center of the braid and around the base of the pot.

# IVY POT

by LeNae Gerig

one 4½" wide terra cotta pot
acrylic paints: ivory, forest green, blue-green
acrylic spray sealer, water-base fruitwood gel stain, clean soft cloth
#0 liner paintbrush, 1" sponge brush
1½" square of compressed sponge, paper plate, paper towels, toothbrush
tracing paper, pencil
**optional:** 1½ cups of green potpourri

1　Lightly sand the pot to remove any rough edges. Spray inside and out with sealer; let dry. Use the sponge brush to paint the pot ivory inside and out; let dry. Trace the ivy leaf pattern and cut from the compressed sponge. Moisten with water to expand the sponge, then squeeze out excess water. Pour a 2" puddle of each green paint onto the paper plate. Dip the sponge into first one paint, then the other. Blot excess on a paper towel and sponge a leaf onto the pot. Repeat to place 9–10 evenly spaced leaves around the pot as shown.

2　Use the liner brush and blue-green to paint vines and curling tendrils among the leaves. Use the brush handle to dip dot (see page 143) groups of three forest green dots among the leaves and vines.

3　Sponge combined greens onto the pot rim as for the ivy leaves; let dry.

4　Moisten the toothbrush and dip it into forest green paint. Use your thumb to pull the bristles back, then release them to spatter paint onto the pot sides. Repeat over the entire pot; let dry. Spray with sealer; let dry. With a soft cloth, rub stain all over the pot to give it an antique look. Let dry and seal again. Line the pot with plastic before putting a plant in it—or fill the pot with potpourri.

# TRINKET BOXES

by Marilyn Gossett

**for each box:**
*acrylic paints: ivory, metallic gold*
*1" sponge brush, 1" square of kitchen sponge*
*paper plate, paper towels*
*tacky craft glue*

**for the ivory & green box:**
*one 3½"x1¾" round papier-mâché box*
*one 1½" square antique gold filigree medallion*
*three 1" wide metallic gold ribbon roses*
*six 2" long sprigs of green preserved plumosus*
*2½ yards of ⅛" wide round ivory cord with gold threads*
*12" of ⅜" wide green/metallic gold flat braid*
*12" of ½" wide green/metallic gold flat braid*

**for the ivory/red/green box:**
*one 3"x1½" round papier-mâché box*
*one 1½" wide red ribbon poinsettia*
*1⅓ yards of ⅛" wide round red/green cord with gold threads*
*10" of ⅜" wide red/metallic gold flat braid*
*10" of ½" wide red/metallic gold flat braid*

1. **For each box:** Use the sponge brush to paint the box and lid ivory, inside and out. Pour a 2" puddle of gold paint onto a paper plate, dip in the sponge square and blot excess on a paper towel. Sponge the gold evenly over the box and lid, letting the ivory show through. Let dry.

2. Apply an even layer of glue to the lid top. Fold in ¼" on one end of the cord and press it into the center. Coil the braid spiral-fashion around the center, keeping the spiral flat and the wraps touching. Trim excess cord, apply glue to the end and tuck it under the previous wrap. Glue ⅜" braid around the rim of the lid.

3. **Green box:** Glue the filigree to the center top of the lid. Glue the roses in a triangle to the center of the filigree. Glue the plumosus under the roses, evenly spaced and extending outward. Glue the remaining cord around the box bottom; glue the ½" braid above the cord.

4. **Red box:** Glue the poinsettia to the center top of the lid. Glue the ½" braid around the bottom of the box.

# HEART & FLOWERS BOX

by Marilyn Gossett

one 5"x1¾"x5" papier-mâché heart box
green/white checked fabric: one 7" square, one 16½"x1¾" piece
1 yard of ½" wide pink floral braid with yellow between the flowers and green leaves
27" of ⅞" wide pink braid with yellow-centered flowers and green leaves
pencil
1" sponge brush
paper plate
tacky craft glue

1 Lay the box lid on the wrong side of a fabric square and trace around it. Cut 1" outside the traced line. Use the sponge brush to apply a thin, even layer of glue all over the top and sides of the lid. Press the fabric onto the top of the box, smooth out any wrinkles, then press it down onto the sides. Let dry, then trim off any excess fabric. Starting at the center top of the heart, glue the fabric strip around the box in the same way.

2 Glue 1" braid from the center top of the lid to the point, wrapping the ends down the sides. Glue another row on each side of the first, positioning it so the flowers almost touch. Repeat with another row on each side. Glue ½" braid around the bottom edge of the box and the bottom edge of the lid.

# BURGUNDY DOILY BOX

by Marilyn Gossett

one 5"x1 ¾"x5" octagonal papier-mâché box
one 4" wide burgundy heart doily
one 1" wide burgundy ruffled ribbon rose
16" of ¾" wide burgundy scalloped flat braid
16" of ⅝" wide green/metallic gold flat braid
7" of ¼" wide green/metallic gold flat braid with
    a ½" wide gold/ivory loop edging
12" of ⅛" wide dark green rope braid
1 yard of ½" wide dark green satin picot ribbon
one 1" tall black/white cameo button
3 assorted ½"–⅝" wide antique gold buttons
one 1" long brass leaf charm
1" sponge brush
1" square of household sponge
paper plate, paper towels
tacky craft glue

1 Use the sponge brush to paint the box and lid ivory, inside and out. Pour a 2" puddle of gold paint onto a paper plate, dip in the sponge square and blot excess on a paper towel. Sponge the gold evenly over the box and lid, letting the ivory show through. Let dry.

2 Glue the burgundy braid around the box bottom. Glue the ⅝" green/gold braid around the lid sides. Glue the doily to the top of the lid, placing the point and each shoulder of the heart at the center of a side.

3 Apply a 1½" circle of glue to the center of the doily. Fold in ¼" on one end of the cord and press it into the center of the glue. Coil the braid spiral-fashion, keeping the spiral flat and the wraps touching. Apply glue to the cord end and tuck it under the previous wrap.

4 Glue the loop braid around the cord circle, loops extending outward. Glue the rose to the cord center, then glue the buttons and charm around the rose as shown in the photo. Use the ribbon to tie a shoestring bow (see page 141) with 1⅜" loops and 5" tails. Glue the bow to the center top of the doily. Loop and glue the tails to the sides as shown.

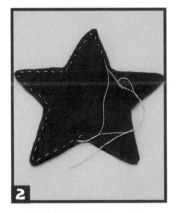

# STAR BOX & COASTERS

by LeNae Gerig

8"x3" papier-mâché star box
gold star charms: one 1½", one ⅞", one ⅝" wide
two 9"x12" pieces of navy blue felt
two 9"x12" pieces of dark green felt
1 yard of 1¾" wide gold mesh wire-edged ribbon
acrylic paints: navy, dark green, gold
natural sea sponge
#12 flat paintbrush
paper towels
needle, metallic gold thread
tracing paper, pencil
24-gauge wire
low temperature glue gun and sticks or tacky craft glue

1 **Coasters:** Trace the bottom of the star box onto the paper and cut out. Use this pattern to cut out four green and four navy felt stars.

2 Sew one green and one navy star together with a running stitch ⅛" from the edge. Repeat for the remaining stars.

3 **Box:** Paint the box and lid gold on the inside, navy on the outside; let dry. Moisten the sponge and dip it into green paint. Blot excess paint on a paper towel, then lightly sponge the outside of the box and lid, allowing navy to show though. Rinse the sponge and repeat with gold paint. Let dry.

4 Use the ribbon to make a puffy bow (see page 141) with a center loop, six 2" loops and no tails. Glue to the center top of the lid. Glue the stars among the loops as shown in the large photo.

Whimsical

118

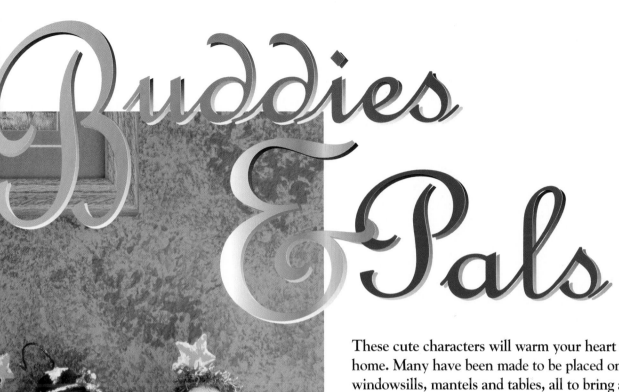

# Buddies & Pals

These cute characters will warm your heart and your home. Many have been made to be placed on shelves, windowsills, mantels and tables, all to bring a special feeling to the home. But many can be made to hang as well, becoming wonderful ornaments for the Christmas tree.

The Sitting Santa on page 120 is perfect for the mantel, carefully watching over the stockings as they're hung with care. Santa's Elf from page 121 holds a shovel in his hands, always the helper Santa needs.

To create more Christmas cheer for the house, there are several snowmen, lovingly and cleverly crafted. The Snow Family on page 122 is perfect when grouped together on a shelf or windowsill, delightfully greeting guests and bringing smiles to faces. Snowmen from clay pots?? These two little guys, found on page 130, are irresistible—and so easy to make!

Lace, ribbons, flowers and fabric are used to create our angels. The Lacy Angel on page 132 is a wonderful gift to be given to someone special while the Two Little Angels on page 124 look splendid decorating the tree or just hanging in that special corner of a home.

This section is brimming with delightful Christmas ornaments, as well as distinctive decorations for the home. Whimsical, cute, pretty, clever, sweet or charming—whatever your taste, we've included buddies and pals to deck your halls, walls and trees!

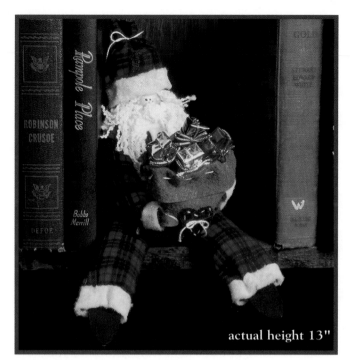

actual height 13"

# SITTING SANTA

by Marilyn Gossett

Santa face

Elf face

**1 Body:** Glue the doll pin into the head, the pin into the stand and the stand to the heart. Paint the top of the stand, pin and head peach. Paint the bottom of the stand and the heart brown. Dip dot (see page 143) black eyes, then use the pen to draw a nose and mouth. Blush the cheeks and dip dot a white highlight on each. Glue two 2" ovals together for a shoe; repeat. Paint the shoes black. Paint the 1½" ovals white for gloves.

**2** Fold the pants leg fabric in thirds lengthwise and glue the raw edge down. Pinch the center and wrap with thread; knot to secure. Lightly stuff with fiberfill and glue batting around each cuff; trim excess batting. Glue the shoes inside the pant legs. Repeat for the arms, but glue in the gloves. Glue to the doll as shown.

**3** Fold the pants fabric in thirds lengthwise and glue the raw edge down. Glue the center of the wrong side to the crotch of the pants legs, then wrap and glue the ends around the stand. Glue the sides together. Glue a ¼" hem in each long edge of the shirt piece. Cut a 1" slit in the center, pull over his head and glue the sides together under the arms. Stuff the shirt lightly with fiberfill.

**4 Fur:** Glue batting around the neck, down the front and around the shirt bottom. Glue the snaps for buttons. **Beard:** Knot the center of the doll hair. Glue the knot below the mouth, spread the strands and glue to secure. Trim to the desired length and glue the trimmings around the sides and back of his head. **Hat:** Glue the short edges together, then glue onto the head. Glue batting around the lower edge. Stuff softly. Tie with thread ½" below the tip, making a shoestring bow (see page 141) with ¾" loops and 1¼" tails. Brush all the fur and the hat with glitter glaze.

one 1¼" round head bead
one 3½" long wooden doll pin with stand
one 1½" wide wooden heart, ⅜" thick
1/16" thick wooden ovals: four 2" long, two 1¼" long
red/black plaid flannel fabric: one 4½"x12" piece (pant legs), 3"x5" piece (pants), 3½"x7" (shirt), 3½"x11" (arms and sleeves), 3"x6" (hat)
one 4"x10" piece of olive green felt (bag)
one 2" square of dark green felt (bag heart)
three ¼" wide black snaps
polyester fiberfill
pink powdered blush, cotton swab
acrylic paints: pale peach, brown, black, white
brush-on glitter glaze
#6 flat paintbrush
four ¾"x1" Christmas packages
fifteen 10" lengths of white Lil' Bumpies™ doll hair
¾"x36" piece of cotton batting
2 yards of white #5 perle cotton thread, needle
black fine-tip permanent pen
low temperature glue gun and sticks or tacky craft glue

**5** **Bag:** Fold the olive felt in half crosswise and sew up each side. Fold the top down 1" and sew a running stitch ¼" below the fold. Lightly stuff the bag; glue the gifts into the top. Cut a heart from dark green felt and sew a running stitch around the outside. Use the remaining thread to tie a shoestring bow with ⅜" loops and 1" tails. Glue to the heart center. Glue the heart to the bag front. Glue the bag in Santa's lap as shown in the large photo on page 120.

# SANTA'S ELF by Marilyn Gossett

actual height 7½"

one 1¼" round head bead
one 3½" long wooden doll pin with stand
1/16" thick wooden shapes: two ⅜" circles, one 1½" square, 1 craft pick
one 2"x¼" wooden heart
green plaid fabric: one 5"x10" rectangle, one 3"x10" rectangle, one ½"x5½" strip
acrylic paints: pale peach, white, black, brown, yellow, green
snow texture paint, satin acrylic sealer, brush-on glitter glaze
black fine-tip permanent pen
paintbrushes: ½" and ⅜" flat, #0 liner
small amount of brown Mini Curl ™ doll hair
red felt: one 4½"x5½" piece (hat), one 2½"x4" piece (collar)
one 1" mini gift box
two ½" round dark green buttons
white #5 perle cotton thread, tracing paper, pencil
low temperature glue gun and sticks or tacky craft glue

collar

**1** Glue the head to the doll pin and the pin to the stand. Glue the stand to the heart as shown. **Ears:** Trim one edge of a ⅜" circle to fit the head and glue in place; repeat on the other side. Paint the pin and head peach, the stand yellow and the heart base brown. Dip dot (see page 143) black eyes and brown freckles (refer to the pattern on page 120). Use the pen to draw the nose and mouth. Blush the cheeks, then dip dot white highlights. Seal the painted pieces.

**2** **Suit:** Sew a running stitch along each long edge of the largest fabric piece. Pull to gather it around the neck and base; secure with glue. Stuff fiberfill through the back seam to fill the body. **Arms:** Fold the rectangle in thirds; glue the raw edge down. Knot the center for hands and glue the ends to the back.

**3** Fluff the hair and glue to his head. **Collar:** Trace the pattern and cut one from red felt. Glue around the neck, seam in back. **Hat:** Follow step 4 on page 120, but use the last fabric strip for trim.

**4** **Sign:** Glue the square to the top of the craft pick. Paint it brown; let dry. Use the pen to draw a dashed line around the edge and to write "Santa's Workshop." Apply snow paint to the top. Glue a button to the collar front and one to the front of the suit as shown in the large photo. Glue the gift box and sign into his arms. Lightly brush glitter glaze onto the hat, collar, suit and snow.

# SNOW FAMILY by Marilyn Gossett

**Dad: 5¾" tall; Mom: 5½" tall; Baby: 3⅜" tall**

acrylic paints: ivory, black, orange, white, yellow
textured snow paint
brush-on glitter glaze
4" round grapevine wreath (1 is enough for all 3 figures)
#4 flat paintbrush
wire cutters, needlenose pliers
polyester fiberfill
pink powdered blush, cotton swab
white thread, needle
20-gauge wire
drill with ⅟16" bit
low temperature glue gun and sticks or tacky craft glue

### for Snowmom or Snowdad:
one 1¼" round wooden head bead
one 3½" long wooden doll pin with stand
one 2" long wooden oval
cotton batting: one 6"x15" rectangle (body), one 2¼"x10"
    piece (arms)
one 1¼" wooden star
⅜" wide wooden plug
1" sprig of dried pink pepperberries

### for Snowdad:
one 1½"x12" piece of red plaid flannel fabric (scarf)
one 2¼"x1" black plastic top hat
one 4½" black plastic cane
one ⅜" black button

### for Snowmom:
12" of acrylic pine
1½"x12" piece of navy blue fabric with gold stars (scarf)

### for Snowbaby:
one 2½" tall doll pin
one 1⅛" wide wooden doll stand
one 1¼" wooden circle
2¼"x6" rectangle of cotton batting
two ⅜" wide red pom poms (ear muffs)
red plaid flannel fabric: one ½"x6" piece (scarf),
    one 1"x2" piece (mittens)

**Baby's mitten**

Dad's or Mom's face

Baby's face

**1** **For each figure:** For Mom or Dad, first glue the bead to the doll pin and the wooden plug for a nose. Glue the pin into the stand. Paint it ivory; let dry. Blush the cheeks and dip dot (see page 143) white highlights. Dip dot black eyes and mouth. Paint the nose orange (use an orange dip dot for Baby).

**2** Sew a running stitch along one long edge of the large cotton batting piece. Pull to gather it around the neck; secure with glue. Repeat to gather the other long edge around the base. Stuff fiberfill through the back seam to fill the body. Sew a running stitch around the waist, 1½" below from the neck. Pull the threads to gather slightly; knot and glue to secure. Glue the oval to the bottom for a stand.

**3** Arms: Fold the 10" batting strip in thirds lengthwise and glue the raw edge down. Knot at the center (hands) and glue the ends behind the shoulders. Cut the bindings from the wreath, pull the wreath apart and wrap around the snowman twice.

**4** **Snowdad:** Wrap the scarf around his neck and knot at his left shoulder. Glue the button to his chest, the hat to his head and the cane into his arms. Glue the pepperberries to the right side of the hat.

**5** **Star:** Drill a hole in one point of the star. Paint the star yellow; let dry. Insert one end of a 10" wire length through the hole and use pliers to twist the end around the wire, securing it. Wrap the wire around a pencil or dowel to coil it, then gently stretch it to separate the coils. Cut a slit in the side of the snowman, below the waist and slightly back of center. Glue the free end of the wire into the opening. Apply snow to the hat, scarf, star and body. Use glitter glaze to sparkle the snow.

**6** **Snowmom:** Wrap the scarf around her neck and knot it at her right. Cut a 4" pine sprig, glue the ends together to form a halo and glue to her head. Wrap the remaining pine into a 2" wide wreath and glue to her hands. Glue berries to the halo and wreath as shown. Follow step 5 to attach a star and apply snow.

**7** **Snowbaby:** Glue a 2" grapevine length to the top of his head, then glue a pom pom to each end to make his earmuffs.

**8** Tie the scarf around his neck with the knot at his right. Trace the mitten pattern and cut it out. Cut one from flannel, then turn over to cut the second. Glue to the body as shown. Brush on snow and glitter glaze as shown in the large photo on page 122.

# TWO LITTLE ANGELS by Marilyn Gossett

drill with ¹⁄₁₆" bit
acrylic paints: pale peach,
    white, brown, black, light
    coral
#4 flat paintbrush
black fine-tip permanent pen
green sheet moss
3½"x4" piece of unbleached
    muslin fabric
20-gauge wire
low temperature glue gun and
    sticks or tacky craft glue

### flying angel:
¹⁄₁₆" thick wooden shapes:
• one 1¼" round
• 1 craft spoon
• three 2" long ovals
• two 1½" long teardrops
• six 2" long teardrops
1⅛ yards of 5" wide ecru flat
    lace with one scalloped edge
green acrylic paint
one 3" long sprig of dried
    German statice
one ½" long pink silk rosebud
two 1½" long sprigs of dried lavender
¾ yard of ¼" wide green satin ribbon

### standing angel:
¹⁄₁₆" thick wooden shapes:
• one 1¼" circle
• 1 craft spoon
• four 1½" long teardrops
• eight 2" long teardrops
22" of 4" wide ivory flat lace
10" of 4" wide ivory flat lace
acrylic paints: turquoise, gray-blue
acrylic crackle medium
three ½" wide pink ribbon roses
¾ yard of ¼" wide pink satin ribbon
ten ½" sprigs of teal preserved baby's breath
twelve ¼" long pink rosebuds

actual width 7"

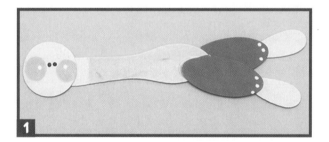

**1** **Flying angel:** Refer to the photo to glue the body parts together. Paint the head and feet pale peach and the bloomers brown. Mix equal parts of water and coral paint to blush the cheeks; let dry. Dip dot (see page 143) black eyes and white cheek highlights. Make three white dip dots on the bottom of each bloomer leg.

**2** Glue three teardrops together in a fan as shown for wings; repeat. Mix equal parts green and water to paint the wings. Paint the remaining oval brown. Use the pen to draw a dashed line around the brown oval. Write "Herbs~" in the oval. Slip: Glue a ¼" hem along each 4" edge of the muslin. Glue it around the angel, finger-gathering the neck, overlapping the raw edges in the back. Glue the back seam.

**3** Dress: Cut a 32" lace length. Sew a running stitch along the straight edge, gather and glue around her neck. Fold the remaining lace into fourths lengthwise, scalloped edge to the front, and knot at the center. Fold the ends under and glue to her back. Tie the ribbon around her waist, knot at the bottom. Glue the wings as shown.

**4** Glue moss to her head and shoulders. Glue the rosebuds and ten statice buds into the moss. Drill two holes 1" apart in the sign, one in her top foot and one in her back wing. Insert one end of a 15" wire length through the wing hole and use pliers to twist the end around the wire, securing it. Wrap the wire around a pencil or dowel to coil it, then gently stretch it to separate the coils. Twist the other end through the foot hole to form the hanger. Use a 5" wire length to make a similar hanger for the sign, looping it through her hands and omitting the coils. Loop and glue the ribbon tails as shown.

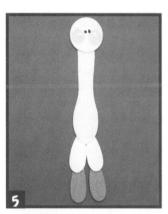

**5** **Standing angel:** Refer to the photo to glue the body parts together. Paint the head peach and the bloomers white; paint the feet and wings turquoise. Follow step 1 to paint the face.

**6** Glue the wings together as shown—make two wings. Let dry, then follow the manufacturer's instructions to apply crackle medium to the wings and feet. Paint the wing centers coral, the rest of the wings and the feet gray-blue; the paint will crackle as it dries. Paint the sign with a half-and half mix of brown paint and water. Use the pen to draw a dashed line around the sign. Write "Garden Angel~" in the oval. Follow step 2 to make the slip.

actual height 6½"

**7** Follow step 3 to make her dress, using pink ribbon in place of the green ribbon. Glue the wings to the back.

**8** Loop and glue the ribbon tails forward as shown. Glue a ribbon rose below her chin and one to each shoe. Glue moss for her hair. Glue the dried rosebuds and baby's breath evenly spaced around the moss. Drill holes in the wing tips and 1" apart in the top of the sign. Follow step 4 to make the hanger and attach the sign.

bear, kitty: 6" tall
bunny: 8" tall

## for each ornament:
brown paper bag
pinking shears or decorative edge scissors
tracing paper, pencil
black fine-tip permanent pen
polyester fiberfill
9" of thin gold cord or nylon monofilament fishing line
pink powdered blush, cotton swab
low temperature glue gun and sticks or tacky craft glue

## for the bear:
brown pom poms: four 1½", three 1", one ¾" wide
one ¼" black bead (nose)
6" of ¼" wide green satin ribbon
red felt pen

## for the kitty:
four 1½" wide tan pom poms
1" square of household sponge
paper towels, paper plate
acrylic paints: ivory, tan
red felt pen
12" of ¼" wide mauve satin ribbon

## for the bunny:
tan pom poms: four 1½", one 1" wide
one ½" wide pink pom pom
6" of nylon monofilament fishing line
12" of ¼" wide pink satin ribbon

# HEART PAL ORNAMENTS

by Marilyn Gossett

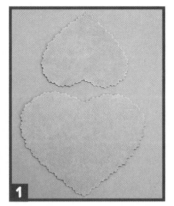
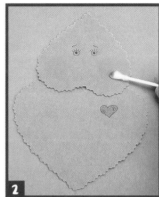

**1** For each ornament: Trace the patterns from page 127. From brown paper, cut out two head and two body hearts. Glue the edges of the head pieces together, leaving a 1" opening for stuffing. Repeat with the body pieces. Cut two ears for the kitty or bunny. Trim each piece with decorative scissors.

**2** Bear: Glue the head to the body as shown. Transfer (see page 143) the face pattern to the head and the small heart pattern to the right side of the chest. Go over the lines with the black pen. Color the heart red. Blush the cheeks.

**3** Stuff each piece lightly with fiberfill, then glue the openings closed. Glue the 1½" pom poms for his arms and legs. Glue a 1" pom pom for each ear and one to the back for a tail.

**4** Glue the ¾" pom pom for his muzzle; glue the bead for the nose. Use the ribbon to make a shoestring bow (see page 141) with ½" loops and ½" tails and glue to the bear's neck. Fold the gold cord in half, knot the ends and glue to the back of the his head for a hanger.

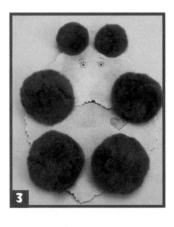

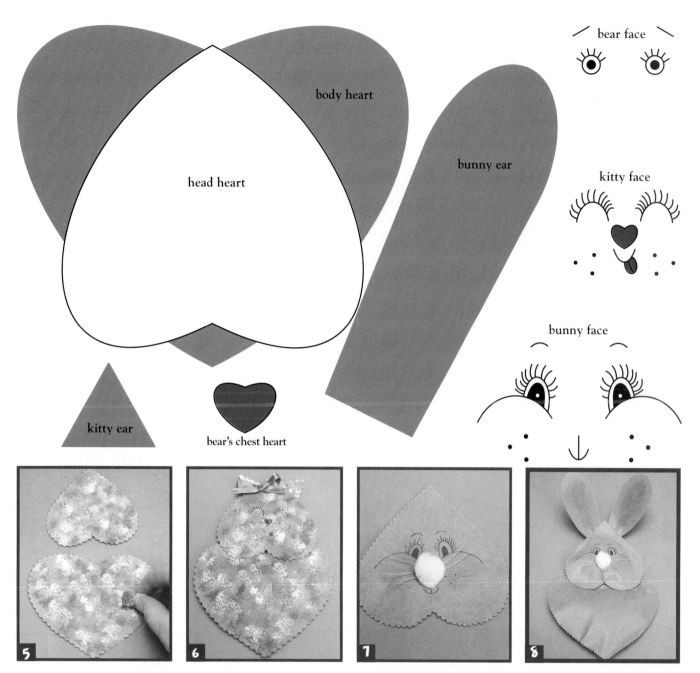

**head heart**

**body heart**

**bunny ear**

**bear face**

**kitty face**

**bunny face**

**kitty ear**

**bear's chest heart**

**5** **Kitty:** Pour a 1" puddle each of tan and ivory paint onto the paper plate. Moisten the sponge, dip it into the tan paint, blot on the paper towel and lightly sponge onto the head and body. Rinse the sponge and repeat with ivory paint. The paper color should show through.

**6** Transfer (see page 143) the face pattern to the head. Go over the lines with the black marker. Color the nose and tongue red. Glue the ears as shown. Cut the ribbon into two 6" lengths and use each to make a shoestring bow with ¾" loops and ¾" tails. Glue one bow to her right ear as shown. Refer to the large photo on page 126 to glue the other bow to her neck and the pom poms for her arms and legs. Fold the gold cord in half, knot the ends and glue to the back of her head for a hanger.

**7** **Bunny:** Transfer (see page 143) the face pattern to the head. Go over the lines with the black marker. Blush the cheeks and glue the pink pom pom for her nose. Cut the nylon line into 1" lengths and glue three on each side of the muzzle for whiskers.

**8** Pinch the base of each ear and glue to the head as shown; blush the inner ears. Glue the head to the body. Cut the ribbon into two 6" lengths and use each to make a shoestring bow with ¾" loops and ¾" tails. Refer to the large photo on page 126 to glue on the bows. Glue the 1½" pom poms for arms and legs and the 1" pom pom for her tail. Fold the gold cord in half, knot the ends and glue to the back of her head for a hanger.

# POSEABLE ANGEL

by Marilyn Gossett

one 14" tall Bendi Doll®
1¾ yards of ⅝" wide pink/gold flat trim
1⅝ yards of ⅛" pink flat trim with ½" gold
　loops
2 yards of ¼" wide pink picot satin ribbon
18"x36" piece of pink net fabric
15 yards of loopy yarn wool hair
seven ⅝" wide white ribbon roses
one 8" round white battenburg lace doily
one 12"x18" white battenburg lace placemat
pink powdered blush, cotton swab
black fine-tip permanent pen
needle, white thread
low temperature glue gun and sticks or tacky
　craft glue

**1** Blush the doll's cheeks; use the pen to draw her mouth and nose. **Slip:** Fold the net in half lengthwise and sew a running stitch along the folded edge. Pull the threads to gather; whipstitch (see page 144) the fold to her waist.

**2** **Dress:** Glue loop trim to the bottom of one short end of the placemat. Glue another row to the scalloped edge where the fabric attaches to the lace. Fold the place mat in half and cut a slit just large enough to fit over the doll's head. Slip it on, then glue the sides together. Bend a 6" loop trim length into a U and glue to the top front of the dress with the loops extending outward and the ends under her chin. Tie 12" of pink trim around the waist, covering the bottom of the bodice trim; knot in the back. **Shoes:** Glue a 2½" piece of pink trim to the bottom of each foot, turning the ends up in the front and back. Glue a 5" length around each foot, overlapping the ends in the back.

**3** **Garland:** Cut two 16" pieces of pink trim. Glue the pieces wrong sides together. Glue one end to one hand, twist three times and glue the other end to the other hand. Glue five ribbon roses evenly spaced along the garland and one to the toe of each shoe. Cut the picot ribbon in half and use each half to make a shoestring bow (see page 141) with 1" loops and 7" tails. Glue one to each hand.

**4** **Hair:** Cut 6" of yarn and set aside. Wrap the remaining yarn loosely around your thumb and fingers 45 times. Slip the yarn off and tie the center with the 6" length. Glue to the doll's head. **Halo:** Glue the ends of a 5" piece of pink trim together to form a circle. Glue the seam to the back of her head so the circle extends upward. **Wings:** Glue 20" of loop trim around the outside of the round doily. Pinch the center and wrap with thread; knot to secure. Glue to the angel's back so the trim faces front.

# POTPOURRI GIRL

## by Marilyn Gossett

¾ yard of ½" wide blue flat braid
⅞ yard of 1" wide white flat tatted lace
1 yard of 1½" wide white organza ribbon with pearl edges
blue ribbon roses: seven ½" wide, one 1" wide
blue/white striped chintz fabric: 5"x11" piece (arms),
    12"x19" piece (skirt)
wooden hearts: one 2", one 3" wide
6½" length of ⅜" wide dowel
one 1½" wooden ball with a ⅜" hole
small handful of blonde curly doll hair
one 4" wide white battenburg heart doily
needle, white #5 perle cotton thread
acrylic paints: peach, blue, black, coral, ivory
#10 flat shader paintbrush
2 oz. of potpourri
drill with ⅜" or ¼" bit (to match dowel for doll body)
low temperature glue gun and glue sticks or tacky craft glue

actual height 8½"

**1** Drill a hole in the middle of the small heart. Glue the dowel into the hole and the ball onto the dowel. Glue the small heart to the large heart; let dry. Paint the hearts ivory, the dowel and head peach. Refer to the pattern to paint the head.

**2** **Skirt:** Fold the large fabric piece in half lengthwise, right sides in. Sew ¼" from each end; turn right side out. Sew lace to the folded edge with braid above it. Pour half the potpourri into the skirt. Sew a running stitch along the raw edge, gather and glue below the head.

**3** **Arms:** Sew lace to each short edge. Fold in half lengthwise, right sides together, and sew ¼" from the raw edge. Turn right side out. Tie thread around the center and glue to her upper back below the head. Lightly fill each sleeve with potpourri; tie the sleeves together.

**4** **Collar:** Cut from the V of the doily to the center and trim to fit around her neck. Glue braid around the edge. Glue the collar in place. Cut the ribbon in half and use each piece to make a shoestring bow (see page 141) with 2½" loops and 3" tails. Glue one to each side of her waist. Glue the hair to her head. Glue the 1" rose in her hair and a rose to the point of the collar. Glue the remaining roses evenly spaced around the skirt hem.

small snowman: 5" tall; large snowman: 7" tall

# CLAY POT SNOWMEN

by Marilyn Gossett

**for each snowman:**
acrylic paints: white, orange
#2 flat paintbrush, sponge brush
fine sandpaper
matte acrylic sealer
textured snow paint, craft stick
brush-on glitter glaze
needle, white thread
pink powdered blush, cotton swab
low temperature glue gun and glue
   sticks or tacky craft glue

**small snowman:**
one 3½"x2½" clay pot
white pom poms: one 1½" (head),
   two 1" (arms), two ½" (hands)
red felt: ¼"x6" strip, ½"x6" strip
black felt: 2½" circle, two
   12"x1½" strips
one ¼" wide wooden plug (nose)
buttons: one ¾" red, three ⅜"
   green, eleven ⅜"–½" white
eight 3mm black half-round beads
   (eyes, mouth)
one 2" long broom

**large snowman:**
one 3½"x3¼" clay pot
white pom poms: one 2½" (head),
   two 1½" (arms)
red felt: ¼"x8" strip, ½"x8" strip
black felt: 3½" circle, two 14"x2"
   strips
one ½" wide wooden plug (nose)
buttons: one ¾" red, three ½"
   green, ten ½"–¾" white
seven 6mm black half-round beads
   (eyes, mouth)

**1** Lightly sand the pot; use the sponge brush to apply sealer. Let dry, then paint the pot white. Invert the pot. Glue the head and arm pom poms as shown.

**2** **Scarf:** Glue the ¼" red felt strip around his neck. Knot the center of the ½" felt strip and glue the knot at one side. **Large snowman's mittens:** Trace the pattern and cut four from red felt. Place two together and sew around the rounded edges with a blanket stitch (see page 144). Repeat. Lightly stuff with fiberfill. Sew a running stitch around the cuff, gather slightly and knot to secure. Glue one mitten to each arm, thumbs up. **Small snowman's hands:** Glue the ½" pom poms to the ends of the arms as shown in the large photo.

**3** **Face:** Paint the wooden plug orange. Glue to the center of the face. Glue the beads for the eyes and nose. Blush the cheeks.

**4** **Hat:** Glue the black felt circle to the snowman's head. Apply glue lengthwise down the center of one black felt strip and roll it into a cylinder. Repeat with the second strip, wrapping it around the first. Glue the cylinder to the center of the circle. Glue a red and a white button to the hat as shown. Glue the green buttons to the body front. Use a craft stick to apply decorative snow to the pot and sparingly to the hat, scarf, etc. Let dry, then glue the white buttons around the pot rim. Apply glitter glaze to the face, hands and scarf. Glue the broom into the small snowman's hand as shown in the large photo.

# SNOWMAN WITH BIRDHOUSE

### by Marilyn Gossett

cotton batting: two 4"x5" pieces (body), one ⅝"x7" strip (arms)
¾"x8" piece of red/black checked fabric (scarf)
green/ ivory plaid fabric: one 3"x3 ½" piece (hat), two ½" squares
     (patches)
one 1" wooden ball with ⅛" hole
1 ½" length of ⅛" wooden dowel
¹⁄₁₆" thick wooden shapes: eight ⅞" long teardrops (birds), two
     ⅞" squares, one 1 ¾" wide triangle (birdhouse)
acrylic paints: ivory, red, dark green, brown, black, gold, orange
paintbrushes: #4 flat, #00 liner
polyester fiberfill, needle, ivory #5 perle cotton thread
round buttons: four ¼" natural, one ⅜" green
round wooden toothpick, 8" length of 18-gauge wire
wire cutters, needlenose pliers, hand drill with ¹⁄₁₆" bit
low temperature glue gun and sticks or tacky craft glue

actual height 5¾"

**1** **Body:** Trace the pattern and cut two from the batting. Place the pieces wrong sides together and sew ⅛" from the outer edges, leaving a ½" opening for the head. Stuff with fiberfill. Knot the center of the arm strip. Glue the ends to the top back.

**2** **Head:** Glue the dowel into the 1" ball. Paint them ivory. **Nose:** Paint one end of the toothpick orange. Drill a ¼" deep hole in the face center. Cut ½" off the painted end of the toothpick and glue into the hole. Blush the cheeks. Dip dot (see page 143) black eyes and a mouth. Glue the neck into the top of the body. **For each bird:** Cut one wooden teardrop in half crosswise; discard the rounded end. Glue the point behind the rounded end of another teardrop, forming a body and tail. Glue the remaining teardrops as shown for wings. Paint one bird black and one red. Paint the beaks gold and dip dot gold eyes. Use the liner with white paint to make broken lines on each bird as shown.

**3** **Birdhouse:** Paint one wooden square red. Use the eraser end of a pencil to dip dot a black door. Use the liner with black to draw broken lines around the edges. Paint the triangle green with white broken lines. Glue to the square for a roof. Drill a hole in the house bottom. Insert one end of the wire and use pliers to twist the end around the wire. Wrap around a pencil to coil it, slip off, then glue the end into the snowman's back so the birdhouse extends at an angle.

**4** **Hat:** Fold up ½" on one long edge. Glue the fold around the top of the head; glue the back seam. Stuff softly and knot a 6" thread length ¾" below the top. Glue the black bird to the knot. Wrap the scarf around his neck and knot at one side. Glue a patch to the scarf. Glue a patch and the green button to the lower right body. Glue the remaining buttons down the center front. **Hanger:** Sew a 6" piece of thread through the hat top and knot the ends. **Feeder:** Paint the second wooden square brown. Glue the red bird to the square, then glue into the snowman's arms. Sparingly apply decorative snow. Brush on glitter glaze.

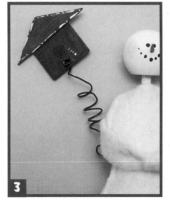

actual height 12"

# LACY ANGEL

by Marilyn Gossett

one 4½" wide wooden heart plaque
9½" length of ⅛" wooden dowel
1 white cotton glove (a left glove was used here)
1 pair of 5¾" wide net/metallic gold wings
six 1" wide red chiffon roses
six 2" sprigs of green preserved princess pine
acrylic paints: pale peach, white, blue
brush-on glitter glaze
#4 flat paintbrush
pink powdered blush, cotton swab
9"x12" piece of white felt
2 yards of 3½" wide white gathered lace
7" of blonde Lil' Loopies™ hair
needle
ivory #5 perle
    cotton thread
drill, ⅛" bit
tracing paper
pencil
polyester fiberfill
low temperature
    glue gun and
    sticks or tacky
    craft glue

**1 Body:** Cut 2½" off the thumb and 2" off the forefinger and little finger of the glove; set aside. Sew the openings closed; sew the remaining thumb to the glove back (see inset photo, page 133 step 1). Turn the knitted cuff inside out and pull out the stitches. Discard the cuff and sew a running stitch around the opening. Softly stuff the glove. **Head:** Stuff the thumb; sew closed. Apply glue to the bottom, insert into the glove and pull up the gathers. Paint the head and hands peach. Dip dot (see page 143) blue eyes. Blush the cheeks.

**2 Sleeves:** Cut two 3"x3½" pieces of white felt. Glue one around each arm. **Shoes:** Trace the pattern and cut four from white felt. Sew two together ⅛" from the edge, leaving the top open. Do not turn. Stuff the foot with fiberfill and glue onto one leg. Repeat for the other foot.

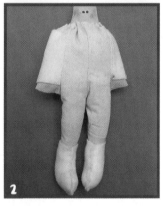

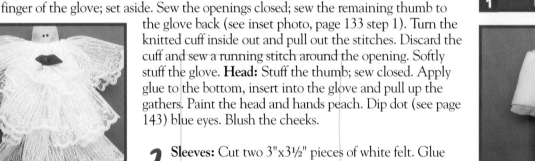

**3 Dress:** Sew a running stitch along the bound edge of a 24" lace length. Gather and glue just above the legs. Repeat with two 12" pieces, gluing one 2½" above the first and the third around her neck. Starting at the center front 1½" below her neck, sew a running stitch through the lace across her front, insert the needle under her arm to the back, sew a running stitch along her back and insert the needle through the other arm. Sew back to the starting point, knot the thread tails to the front and glue a rose to the knot.

back view

**4 Hair:** Cut off one strand and tie around the center of the remaining hair. Glue to her head. Trim a few strands and glue for bangs. **Halo:** Glue four pine sprigs around her head as shown. Glue four roses ½" apart to the halo. Glue the remaining pine to one hand; glue a rose to the top. Glue on her wings. **Stand:** Drill a hole in the heart center, glue in the dowel and paint the stand white. Make a small opening in the angel's bottom and push the dowel into it. Lightly brush glitter glaze over the entire angel.

# FLOWER GIRL

### by Marilyn Gossett

*1 white cotton work glove (a right glove was used here)*
*felt: 5"x6" piece of yellow, 5" square*
*    of white, 7" square of dark green*
*one 7½" long shovel*
*paintbrushes: ¼" and ½" flat*
*acrylic paints: pale peach, white, blue, dark green, black*
*brush-on glitter glaze*
*tracing paper, pencil*
*needle, white thread, green #5 perle cotton thread*
*low temperature glue gun and sticks or tacky craft glue*

**1** **Body:** Cut 2½" of the thumb, 2" of the forefinger and 2" of the little finger off the glove; set aside. Turn the remaining thumb to the back of the glove and sew down (see inset); sew the finger openings closed. Cut off and discard the cuff. Stuff the glove with fiberfill. **Head:** Stuff the thumb and sew it closed. Apply glue around the bottom and insert into the glove top. Sew a running stitch around the glove. Pull the threads to gather the cuff around the neck; knot to secure. **Hands:** Stuff and sew the fingers as for the head; set aside.

**2** Paint the head, hands and legs peach, the body and arms white—extend the white into each hand where the button will go (see step 3). Transfer (see page 143) the face and shoe patterns. Paint the shoes green; dip dot (see page 143) a white button on the outside of each. Go over the face with the pen, blush the cheeks and dip dot white highlights.

**3** Paint the bottom 2½" of the body in a checkerboard pattern. Use the ½" brush to paint ½" long strokes ½" apart. Use the ¼" brush and make ¼" strokes for the sleeve checkerboards. Use the pen to draw a dashed stitching line along the bottom of each sleeve. Draw a circle for the button and dot two holes. Draw a stitching line along the top of each shoe and around each shoe opening. Glue the top of a sleeve to each shoulder, placing them so the buttons are outward—do not glue down the hands.

**4** **Flower:** Trace the patterns. Cut six rounded petals from white felt and seven pointed petals from yellow felt. Sew a running stitch along the bottom of each petal, gather to ½" wide and knot. Glue the yellow petals evenly spaced around the face. Glue the white petals between the yellow ones. **Wings:** Trace the pattern. Cut two from green felt, placing the dashed line of the pattern on the fold of the felt. Unfold and place one wing on the other. Sew together with perle cotton, making ¾" long blanket stitches (see page 144). Sew a running stitch across the center. Glue the wings to the her back. Brush the entire girl with glitter glaze. Glue the spade into her hands as shown in the large photo.

actual height 10"

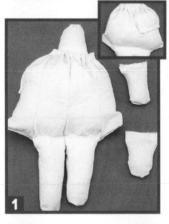

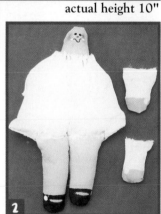

actual height 4"

# GARDEN ANGEL PIN

by Marilyn Gossett

*one 3" long finger from a cotton glove*
*green/ivory/burgundy plaid fabric:*
  *2½"x3¼" piece (dress), ½"x10"*
  *strip (arms)*
*seven 1" sprigs of yellow dried yarrow*
*two ¼" long pink dried rosebuds*
*five 1" long sprigs of dried purple*
  *larkspur*
*two ¾" wide yellow silk black-eyed*
  *Susan blossoms*
*handful of Spanish moss*
*polyester fiberfill*
*1½" long pin back*
*ivory #5 perle cotton thread, needle*
*black fine-tip permanent pen*
*brush-on glitter glaze*
*low temperature glue gun and sticks*
  *or tacky craft glue*

**1** Stuff the glove finger with fiberfill. Glue the opening closed. Use the pen to draw the facial features; blush the cheeks.

**2 Dress:** Glue the 2½"x3¼" fabric piece around the doll, one long edge 1" down from the top of the head. Overlap the short edges in the back and glue the seam. Beginning at the center front, sew a running stitch around the top edge of the dress, leaving a 4" tail of thread on each side. Pull the thread ends tight, knot, then tie a shoestring bow (see page 141) with 1½" loops and 3" tails. Glue a black-eyed Susan, a yarrow and a single larkspur blossom to the bow.

**3 Hair:** Glue moss to her head. **Halo:** Glue the yarrow evenly spaced around her head. Repeat with the remaining flowers.

**4 Wings:** Fold the fabric strip in half lengthwise and glue the raw edges together; let dry. Form into two loops, crossing the ends as shown, and glue to her back. Glue on the pin back. Brush glitter glaze lightly over the angel. (For an ornament, omit the pin back. Before step 3, sew a 5" length of thread through the top of her head and knot the ends together.)

ear

carrot

# LETTUCE BE FRIENDS

### by Jackie Zars

one 1⅝" long wooden doll peg
one 1¼"x¼" wooden bucket
1" length of green jute twine
2"x3" piece of light green paper ribbon
two ¼" balls of orange polymer clay
1½" tuft of Spanish moss
acrylic paints: brown, white
white dimensional paint
pink powdered blush
cotton swab
#6 flat paintbrush
1"x¾" piece of white paper
decorative paper edgers or pinking shears
black fine-tip permanent pen
1"x3" piece of white muslin fabric
tracing paper, pencil
low temperature glue gun and sticks or tacky craft glue

LETTUCE be FRIENDS

actual height 3½"

**1** **Bucket:** Mix equal parts of brown paint and water to paint the bucket; let dry. Trim the paper with the edgers, then transfer (see page 143) "LETTUCE BE FRIENDS" to the paper and go over the lines with the pen. Glue to the bucket front. Fill the basket with moss.

**2** **Bunny:** Paint the peg white. Transfer the face pattern, go over the lines with the pen and blush the cheeks. Use the dimensional paint to squeeze a dot onto each cheek; let dry. Trace the ear pattern, cut two ears from white felt and blush the inner ears. Glue as shown; glue the bunny into the bucket back.

**3** **Lettuce:** Cut the paper ribbon into two 1"x2" strips. Accordion fold the strips crosswise, then fold each piece in half lengthwise and glue into the bucket.

**4** **Carrots:** Roll each clay ball into a ⅝" long cone. Use a pencil to make a hole at the blunt end and the knife to draw creases. Bake at 250° for 30 minutes; let cool. Cut the jute into ¼" lengths and glue into the holes; fray the ends to resemble carrot tops. Glue into the bucket as shown in the large photo.

# SWEET LITTLE DOLL by Loyal Hjelmervik

actual height 5"

leg

one 2½" tall wooden doll peg
two ½" round wooden beads
7" square of white muslin fabric
10" square of green/white checked fabric
⅓ yard of ½" wide ivory gathered lace
⅔ yard of ⅛" wide green satin ribbon
⅓ yard of ⅛" wide white satin ribbon
strawberry blonde Mini Curl™ curly hair
one ⅜" wide pink ribbon rose with green leaves
5½" length of white chenille stem
two ¼" wide clear buttons
black acrylic paint, #6 flat paintbrush
drill with a 1/16" bit
tracing paper, pencil
sewing machine, hand needle, white thread
pink powdered blush, cotton swab
black fine-tip permanent pen
polyester fiberfill
low temperature glue gun and sticks or tacky craft glue

**1 Legs:** Drill a hole crosswise through the peg ¼" from the bottom. Trace the patterns. Cut four leg pieces from muslin. Place two together and sew with a ¼" seam; leave the top open. Clip the curves, turn right side out and stuff firmly. Turn under ¼" on the top and sew the opening closed. Repeat for the other leg. Place one leg on each side of the peg with the top ¼" above the hole. Place a button over each hole. With doubled thread, sew several times back and forth through the buttons, fabric and hole.

**2** Paint the bottom 1" of the feet black; let dry. Tie 9" of green ribbon around each ankle in a shoe-string bow with ⅜" loops and ⅜" tails. Glue the center of the chenille length at the back of the neck. Glue the beads onto the ends for hands. Use the pen to dot eyes.

**3** Cut the dress pattern twice on the fold of the green fabric. Place the pieces right sides together; sew each side/arm in a ¼" seam. Sew the shoulders, leaving a 6" opening for the neck. Clip the corners and turn right side out. Turn under a ¼" hem at the bottom. Place the bound edge of the lace behind the hem and sew ⅛" from the fold. Turn under a ¼" hem on each sleeve and sew a gathering stitch ⅛" from the fold. Put the dress on the doll, pull the thread to gather each sleeve around the wrist, and knot to secure.

**4** Tie the white ribbon around her neck in a shoestring bow with ½" loops and 3" tails. Cut the hair into 2" lengths and glue to the head, working from back to front. Trim the front hair into bangs. Use the green ribbon to make a shoestring bow with ⅜" loops and ⅜" tails; glue to her left hair. Blush her cheeks and glue the ribbon rose in her right hand as shown in the large photo.

1

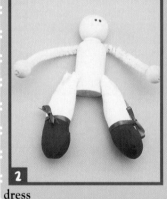

2

dress

3

4

# CAROLING MOUSE

by Teresa Nelson

tan pom poms: two 1½" (body and head), four ¾" (arms
　　and legs), two ¼" (muzzle)
one 6mm black round bead (nose)
two 4mm half-round beads (eyes)
2"x5" piece of tan felt (ears and tail)
1"x2" piece of pink felt (inner ears)
3" square of white felt (wings)
9" of 1½" wide ivory gathered lace
12" of ¹⁄₁₆" wide burgundy satin ribbon
6" of fine gold cord (hanger)
1"x2" piece of thick white paper (book)
3" of 4mm ivory fused pearls
black fine-tip permanent pen
needle, ivory thread
tracing paper, pencil
low temperature glue gun and sticks or tacky craft glue

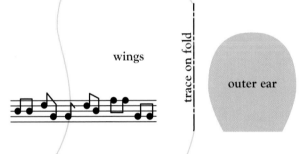

inner ear

wings

trace on fold

outer ear

tail

actual height 2¾"

**1** **Mouse:** Glue the pom poms together as shown; do not glue on the hands. Glue the beads for the eyes and nose.

**2** Sew a running stitch along the bound edge of the lace. Pull to gather it around the mouse's neck. Knot and trim the thread. Glue the hand pom poms over the lace.

**3** Trace the patterns. Cut a pair of wings from white felt, a tail and two ears from tan felt, and two inner ears from pink felt. Glue the tail in place. Glue an inner ear on the center bottom of each tan ear. Pinch the

base and glue to the head. Form the pearls into a circle, glue the ends and slip them over an ear; glue in place.

**4** Glue the wings to the mouse's back. Cut the ribbon in half and use each piece to tie a shoestring bow (see page 141) with ½" loops and ½" tails. Glue one to the center of the wings. Glue the other under her chin. **Music:** Fold the white paper in half crosswise. Write "Silent Night" on the front. Transfer (see page 143) the music to the back and inside; go over the lines with the pen. Glue to the hands. Knot the cord ends together and glue to the back of her head for a hanger.

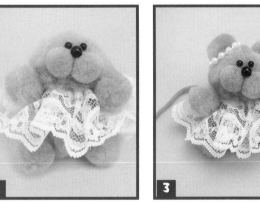

back view

4½" tall including candle

# LITTLE LAMB & CANDLE

by Nancy Overmyer

*dough (see page 142): natural, pink*
*9" of ⅛" wide pink satin ribbon*
*2" tall wooden thread spool*
*blue/white spiral birthday candle*
*acrylic paints: blue, pink, black, cream*
*satin acrylic varnish*
*#2 flat paintbrush*
*round wooden toothpick*
*4" square of aluminum foil*
*knife*
*garlic press*
*low temperature glue gun*
*   and sticks or tacky*
*   craft glue*

lamb body

**1  Lamb:** Fill the garlic press with natural dough. Press out a ⅛" length. With the toothpick, lift it off and place it on foil. Repeat to fill a space the size of the body pattern with dough strands. Roll a ⅜" ball of natural dough for the head. Moisten the neck area with water and press the head in place. Use the knife to imprint a line for the mouth.

**2**  Squeeze out ⅛" more dough and attach a tuft to the top of the head. Roll a ⅛" ball of natural dough into a teardrop for the ear. Gently flatten, dip one end in water and attach to the head. **Feet:** Roll a ¼" ball of natural dough into a smooth oval and cut in half. Dip the top of each half in water and attach to the body as shown.

**3  Heart:** Gently flatten a ⅛" ball of pink dough. Pinch the bottom to a point and use the toothpick to make a dent in the top. Moisten with water and attach to the body as shown. Bake at 300° until hard (about 20 minutes). Let cool; seal (see page 142).

**4  Spool:** Paint blue; let dry. Use the toothpick to make white dip dots (see page 143) around the top and bottom rims, staggering them as shown. Let dry; seal. Glue the sealed lamb to one side of the spool. Make a black dip dot for its eye. Insert the candle in the hole of the spool. Use the ribbon to make a shoestring bow (see page 141) with ¾" loops and 1" tails. Glue to the candle base.

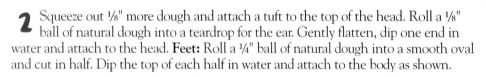

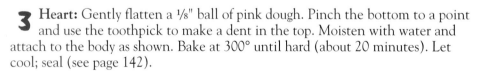

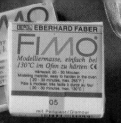

# Hints, Tips & Techniques

# Collar Bow

**1** Form a ribbon length into a circle, crossing the ends in front. Pinch to form a bow; adjust the loop size and tail length. If no tails are needed, just barely overlap the ends before pinching into a bow.

**2** Wrap the center with wire and twist tightly at the back to secure. Trim the wire ends, then wrap a short ribbon length over the wire and glue at the back. Cut each tail diagonally or in an inverted V.

# Loopy Bow

This loopy bow has a center loop.

**1** Measure the desired tail length from the end of the ribbon and make a loop on each side of your thumb. If a center loop is needed, measure the desired tail length from the end of the ribbon and make the center loop before the bow loops.

**2** Continue making loops on each side of your thumb until the desired number is reached (for a ten-loop bow, make five loops on each side).

**3** Wrap the center with wire and twist tightly at the back to secure. If a center loop was made, insert the wire through it before twisting the ends at the back. Trim the wire ends. Cut each tail diagonally. Another method of securing the bow is to wrap a length of ribbon or cord around the center and tie it at the back—this also adds a second set of tails.

# Oblong Bow

**1** Form a center loop by wrapping the ribbon around your thumb. Twist the ribbon a half turn to keep the right side showing, then make a loop on one side of the center loop.

**2** Make another half twist and another loop on the other side. Make another half twist and form a slightly longer loop on each side of your hand; notice these loops are placed diagonally to the first loops.

**3** Make two more twists and loops on the opposite diagonal. Continue for the desired number of loops, making each set slightly longer than the last set.

**4** **For tails:** Bring the ribbon end up and hold in place under the bow. Insert a wire through the center loop, bring the ends to the back and twist tightly to secure. Trim each tail diagonally or in an inverted V.

# Puffy Bow

**1** If a center loop is required, begin with one end of the ribbon length and make the center loop. Twist the ribbon to keep the right side showing. If no center loop is called for, begin with step 2.

**2** Make a loop on one side of your thumb. Give the ribbon a twist and make another loop on the other side of your thumb. Continue making loops and twists until the desired number is reached (a ten-loop bow has five loops on each side), ending with a twist.

**3** **For tails:** Follow step 4 of the Oblong Bow on page 140.

# Shoestring Bow

**1** Measure the desired tail length from the end of the ribbon, then make a loop of the specified length. Wrap the free end of the ribbon loosely around the center of the bow.

**2** Form a loop in the free end of the ribbon and push it through the center loop. Pull the loops in opposite directions to tighten, then pull on the tails to adjust the size of the loops. Trim each tail diagonally or in an inverted V.

# Ribbon Rose

**1** Fold the right ribbon end down diagonally.

**2** Tightly roll the ribbon two turns to the left, then fold the right end back and down.

**3** Continue to roll and fold until there is only a 1" tail remaining on the left.

**4** Hold the tails together and wrap with a 5" wire length. Twist the wire ends together; trim the ends.

# Working with Dough Art

## The Very Best Dough Recipe:
2 cups flour (bleached or unbleached; not self-rising)
½ cup plain or iodized salt
¾ cup hot water (as it comes from the tap)

Pour the hot water and salt into a bowl and stir for one minute. The salt grains will reduce in size, but not dissolve. Add the flour and stir until the water is absorbed.

(It is a good idea to remove your rings before this step.) Turn the dough onto a table or bread board and knead for a few minutes. When the dough is smooth and pliable, it is ready to use. Keep it in a plastic bag so it will not dry out as you work. It's best to use it within 24 hours.

This recipe may be halved, doubled or tripled.

**For colored dough:** Add liquid tempera paint to the water before mixing. When the water is the desired shade, the dough will turn out the same color. Mix as directed above.

## Sealing Baked Pieces:
After baking and painting, all dough pieces should be sealed to prevent them from drawing moisture from the air. Spray or brush-on acrylic sealers will work; however, the pieces in this book were sealed with a polymer coating which dries to a clear, hard, durable shine. To use this method you will need:

*2-part polymer sealer (EnviroTex Lite® or Ultra-Glo)*
*rubber gloves, apron*
*newspapers, large paper clips, hand-held hair dryer*
*plastic spoons, disposable aluminum pie tin*
*cardboard box, wooden dowels long enough to fit across the box*

## Joining Dough Pieces:
Dip your finger into clean water and moisten the areas which are to be joined. Gently press the moistened areas together. Do **not** smooth the joined area or add water over the piece.

## Baking:
Note: If you create each ornament on a piece of aluminum foil torn to size, you can lift the foil to easily transfer the ornament onto a baking sheet. Preheat your oven to 325°. Place the dough on a baking sheet and bake until completely hard (1–1½ hours for most of the pieces in this book). Test by pressing on the thickest part; if it gives at all, bake longer. Do not bake too long, or the dough may burn.

## Two Ways to Make a Hanger:
Use wire cutters to cut paper clips in half (this will make three hangers). Or cut a 1½" length of 18-gauge wire, bend it into a loop and twist the ends together. Insert into the top of the ornament before baking, leaving ⅛"–¼" extending.

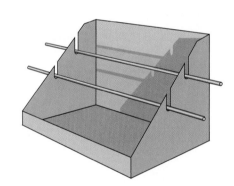

**1** Begin by making a drying rack—the size depends on the number of ornaments you want to seal at one time. Cut a cardboard box diagonally as shown, leaving a lip at the front edge. Cut vertical slots 3"–4" apart along the sides and insert the dowels. Line the bottom with newspapers.

**2** Straighten several large paper clips as shown—you will need one for each ornament. Hook one end through the ornament hanger. Handle the ornament by the paper clip while you seal  it, then hook the clip over a dowel to suspend the ornament while it dries.

**3** Spread newspapers to protect your work surface, protect your clothing with an apron, and wear rubber gloves to mix and apply the sealer. Pour resin into a plastic cup and an equal amount of hardener into another. Pour the hardener into the resin and stir with a spoon until the mixture bubbles. Lay an ornament in the pie tin and pour sealer over it. With your gloved fingers, scoop sealer from the tin to cover the entire ornament, front and back. Work the sealer into any grooves and details.

**4** Hang the ornament on the drying rack. Heat it with the hair dryer on the low setting to pop bubbles and prevent them from drying in the resin. Let the ornament set for about 2½ hours (less if the room is warm), then lift it by the paper clip and use a toothpick to wipe off any drips. Hang again for 6–8 hours to finish curing.

# Working with Polymer Clays

Polymer clays are plastic compounds which can be handled and molded like traditional clays, then hardened in a home oven. Some of the brands available are Fimo®, Sculpey®, Friendly Clay™ and Cernit®. They come in many colors, and the cured clay can be painted with acrylic paints. Some hints on working with these clays:

**Cleanliness is important:** A plastic laminate (Formica®) countertop or table makes a good work surface. Optional: Tape down a sheet of oven parchment or waxed paper to work on; replace it when it becomes stained. Clean your hands, tools and work surface before and after every project, and between colors. Baby wipes are great for this!

Keep your clay and kitchen equipment separate—once a tool has been used for polymer clay it should not be used for food preparation. Do not eat while working with clay (this keeps crumbs out of your clay and clay out of you).

**Softening and kneading:** Some polymer clays are ready to use right out of the package; others must be softened first. Cut the clay into small pieces and knead first one, then add the next. Warm between your hands or in a plastic bag in your pocket to speed the softening process. Even ready-to-use clays will need a little kneading to reach a workable "body temperature" and pliability.

**Using patterns:** You can: (1) Tape waxed paper or oven parchment over the page and shape the clay on it or (2) trace the pattern onto paper, cut it out, lay the paper on a sheet of clay and cut around it.

**Baking:** Always preheat your oven and test with a separate oven thermometer for accurate temperature. Too hot an oven will burn the clay, especially whites and pastels. Different brands of clay require slightly different temperatures, so be sure to check the manufacturer's baking instructions. Line your baking pan with oven parchment or a piece of brown paper bag to prevent shiny spots. Bake for the specified time (about 20 minutes for each ¼" of thickness), then turn off the oven and allow to cool before touching the clay. The clay hardens as it cools. Do not microwave polymer clays!

**Ornament hangers:** See page 142.

# Transferring Patterns

First trace the pattern from this book onto tracing paper. Use dark transfer paper for light surfaces and white transfer paper on dark surfaces. Lay the transfer paper shiny side down on the surface and place the tracing paper over it— secure with masking tape if necessary. Go over the lines again with the pencil or a stylus to transfer them. After painting, a damp cloth or artist's eraser can be used to remove any lines that are still visible.

# Decorative Painting Tips

**Acrylic paints** are available in a wide range of colors from many manufacturers. They dry quickly, can be thinned with water, and brushes can be cleaned with soap or dishwashing detergent and water.

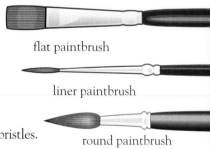

flat paintbrush

liner paintbrush

round paintbrush

Use a brush appropriate to the size of the area to be covered—large flat brushes are best for big areas. Smaller round or liner brushes work better for detail painting. Take care of your brushes—clean them after use and leave them bristles up to dry. Never let paint dry in the bristles.

**Dip dots:** An easy way to make perfect dots for eyes, etc. is to dip the handle end of a paintbrush in the paint and touch it to the surface. Hold the brush vertical for a perfectly round dot. Make 2–3 dots before redipping the brush—they will decrease in size. Use a round wooden toothpick for small dots.

**Dimensional paints** (see illustration at left) are meant to be squeezed on. They dry to a rounded or ridged "dimensional" appearance. Before using a bottle of dimensional paint, hold it tip downward and shake the paint into the tip to prevent air bubbles. For smooth lines, squeeze gently and move the tip along just above the surface—the faster you move, the thinner the line will be. To make perfectly round dots, hold the bottle vertically and squeeze out the desired amount of paint, then stop squeezing and lift the bottle straight up.

# Working with Florals
## Flower Measurements:

When a **length** is given, measure from the flower top to the stem end.

When a **blossom length** is given, measure only the blossom.

When a **stem length** is given, measure only the stem.

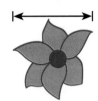

When a **blossom width** is given, measure the open flower head.

## Floral Tape & Wood Picks:

Waxy floral tape is used to lengthen or reinforce stems. Hold the stem together with a wood pick or a length of 18-gauge wire and wrap both spiral-fashion with floral tape, gently stretching the tape so that it adheres to itself.

Floral tape is also used to join stems into clusters, as well as to cover and hide structural wires or other materials.

Wired wood picks come with lightweight wire attached, and are also used for lengthening and reinforcing. The flower stem or cluster is held near the top of the pick, then the wires are wrapped around both to secure them.

## Wire Loop Hangers:

Insert a 6" length of 20-gauge wire into the center top of the project. Twist the ends together, forming a loop.

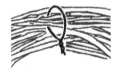

## Stems & Sprigs:

A "**stem**" refers to an entire stem of flowers as purchased. When cut apart, individual pieces become "**sprigs**" to be inserted into a design.

## Gluing:

To prevent flowers from shifting or falling out, coat the ends with glue before inserting. Tacky craft glue effectively secures stems in floral foam. Dip the cut stem in glue, then insert it into the foam. If you use tacky glue you can, while the glue is still wet, pull out a too-long stem, trim and reinsert it without destroying the foam.

Hot or low temperature glue guns are handy for floral designing and the glue is quicker to harden than tacky craft glue. The low temperature glue is safer, but is not as secure as hot glue when used on items preserved with glycerine. Apply glue to the stem end, then insert; hold in place until the glue has set.

**Warning:** Extreme care must be exercised whenever using a glue gun or pan, as burns may result. Never leave a child unattended with hot or low temperature glue.

---

# Sewing Stitches

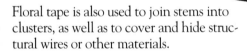

**Running stitch:** Insert the needle into the fabric, then bring it out again 1/16"–1/4" away. Long running stitches are used for gathering or basting. Short running stitches are used to join fabric layers.

**Blanket stitch:** Insert the needle down through the fabric 1/4"–1/2" from the edge. Bring it up at the edge, making sure the thread is wrapped under the needle. Pull taut, then insert the needle down through the fabric 1/4"–1/2" away from the first insertion. Bring it up at the edge with the thread under it. Repeat along the fabric edge. The thicker the fabric, the longer and deeper the stitches.

**Whipstitch:** (Primarily used to close openings.) Insert the needle at an angle through both layers. Bring it out and around the edge, then reinsert at the same angle.